THIS FLAG DOES NOT COME DOWN

ART EVANS

It's my joy to dedicate this book to my wife, Wendy.

Without this precious gift from God to me, I'm quite sure,
I wouldn't be alive to have written this book.

Wendy, your unshakable love, enduring
(frankly, mindboggling) patience,
and relentless kindness have, more times than I can remember,
lent me courage, strength, and resolve to face and defeat many pirates.

Thank you.

Contents

PREFACE

"I will straight-up embarrass you!" the pirate threatened. "You're not gonna say anything to anyone, or I will shame you to your grave!"

Anytime I considered telling you my story, the thug, who controlled my life for far too many years, would reimpose this impending warning. He'd remind me of my weaknesses, many failings, and deplorable base-behavior. I've kept it buried for decades.

One day, while preparing to preach to the precious people I was privileged to be pastoring, I heard the voice of God speak to my heart. "Rather than telling people about what you've done in your life, why don't you tell them about what I've done in your life?"

In response, I've written this book.

Pastoring for 32 years, taught me that my journey, even though different from yours, is a story not unlike yours. I've grown to understand that telling others about God's pursuit of my heart may encourage and inspire trust in His unwavering love and war-readiness on our behalf. It's a tribute to our Creator's extraordinary mercies, faithfulness, and unstoppable power.

My hope is that my story is far more about the Prince of Life than the Prince of Pirates.

The divine manifest for our lives is beyond valuable, as you will see. It frames our gifts, our relationships, journey, assignments, and ultimately, our final destination. Like many, my manifest was destroyed by the pirates who commandeered my life. Furthermore, by the pirates driving my ship and the fierceness of the storms of my life, without the plan and power of the Captain of my Salvation onboard my vessel, I spent years wandering through the vast and often dark seas of this world.

"But God, Who is rich in mercy...

1

As I've spent many hours recalling different seasons of my life, I remember so many people who've helped me navigate my course. My parents, Ken and Carol Evans, my sister, Jenna Coy Davenport, and my brother, Ken, cultivated an environment where, even in my dreadful days, I felt safe. Many coaches, teachers, pastors, and friends don't realize how much each one has enriched my life.

I can't begin to say enough about my wife, Wendy, whom God used to save my life, and, more times than I can remember, keep me on my course.

Dear Reader, when all was lost, *Jehovah Nissi*, the Lord our Banner, answered back to the cry of my heart. He stepped onto my ship, delivered me from the hands of the pirates, restored my manifest, and has promised me a place in His forever-family. I'm eternally grateful.

I'm a living testimony of Jesus' love, grace, and saving power. I believe with all of my heart, what He has done for me, He will do for anyone who will trust Him. I hope my story will assure or reassure you of His tireless pursuit to raise His flag over your life.

- Art Evans
Shreveport, Louisiana
www.artevans.com

INTRODUCTION

"Sir! Sir!" the horror-struck barrelman caterwauled, bursting into the quiet lantern-lit quarters of his captain.

"Worthy news or yer head, youngin'! T'day hadn't even started yet."

"Upon your p-pardon, sir! There are fi-fi-five of 'em!" The young deckhand quickly turned the lamp dial to brighten the cabin. "One is massive! All are wavin' the r-r-rags o' death!"

William Wyer, captain of the *Protestant Caesar*, frantically pulled on his musty boots and ratty coat. Snatching his spyglass, he stumbled up the stairs from his cabin and onto the open poop deck, made exceptionally slick by the thick morning fog on the Bay of Honduras. Dawn offered barely enough light to see over the rolling billows. Rubbing and blinking vigorously, he did all he could to clear his crusty eyes.

What he saw snatched his breath away.

Is this a dream?

Dread shot to his core, instantly vaporizing the grogginess of his lingering stupor. Breath suspended, he melded the brass ring of his "bring 'em near" to his right eye. Peering across the quiet and confining cove, he felt his heart drumming in his ears, an instinctive rhythm of panic.

A seasoned Caribbean sea captain, Wyer had faced and defeated plenty of pirates. But this was no run-of-the-mill robber. This was the Prince of Pirates!

Blackbeard's flagship, *Queen Anne's Revenge*, flanked by four well-weaponed sloops, oozed from the mist and drifted to a rest, rendering the narrow inlet inescapable. Hoping he was mistaken, the distraught captain raised his telescope to confirm the colors flying on the mainmast

3

of the terrible ship. Sinking in solitude, he stared down the dark tunnel of his spyglass, through the cracked and hazy lens, to the bone-melting realization of his worst nightmare. Numbed, he bit down hard on the inside of his cheek, trying to divert his anguish.

Blackbeard's Flag: A black background flaunting a horned skeleton holding, in one hand, a spear, piercing a heart that is dripping blood, and in the other, an hourglass. In a phrase: Torture and death, without mercy, have come, and you are out of time.

A whisper of the name Blackbeard struck fear into the hearts of sea skippers. Notoriety of the criminal Kraken had clouded the Caribbean skies and imaginations for some time. Captain Wyer was no exception to the threats of the no-bluffs bully. Edward Teach (Blackbeard's given name) bolstered his bewitching malevolent mystic at every turn with acts of cruelty and savagery. Like the pearl handle of his cutlass, he polished it with an image projecting pure evil.

> *Teach's actions also contributed to his reputation as a monster. He disemboweled captives and fed their entrails to the sharks. He cut off the fingers of victims who were too slow to hand over their rings. He sliced up a prisoner's ears—and then forced him to eat them. What's more, he turned on his crew with no forewarning. He shot randomly at the pirates on his ship and marooned them when he didn't feel like sharing the bounty. Although there's no telling where the facts end and legend begins, it is probably safe to say that Blackbeard deserved his reputation as "the devil's brother."*[1]

If that wasn't enough, his beard was the deepest black, knotted and craggy. Like a mask to cover the shame of it all, Edward Teach's beard grew from just below the sockets of his dark and malignant eyes to an extraordinary length. It was thick and broad and braided with bone. This dread-inducing trademark earned him the moniker Captain Blackbeard.

Blackbeard was said to frighten his opponents just by looking at them. To add to the intrigue and fear, Blackbeard was rumored to have woven gunpowder-laced wicks into his beard and lit them when he went into battle. The description of this "demon from hell" look, partly corroborated by eyewitness accounts of the time, outdoes anything that Hollywood could invent: "our Heroe, Captain Teach, assumed the cognomen of Blackbeard, from that large quantity of hair, which, like a frightful meteor, covered his whole face ... his beard was black, which he suffered to grow of an extravagant length ... he was accustomed to twist it with ribbons, in small tails ...and turn them about his ears. In time of action, he wore a sling over his shoulders, with three braces of pistols, hanging in holsters like bandoliers; and stuck lighted matches under his hat, which appearing on each side of his face, his eyes naturally looking fierce and wild, made him altogether such a figure, that imagination cannot form an idea of a fury, from hell, to look more frightful. This, combined with his well-armed flagship, would strike fear into the heart of any man.[2]

Long, thick, greasy, pitch-black hair scattered in every direction from underneath his tallish leather tricorne. Hanging from the shoulders of his towering six-foot-five-inch frame was a solid-black, full-length coat. His boots came up to his knees. Captain Blackbeard was an ominous figure of awe, a bedeviling prophet of pending doom.

With five ships, eighty guns, and well over four hundred well-rested ready-to-rumble ranks, all was in the pirate's favor.

"Raise the dead, boy!" Wyer commanded the wide-eyed watchman. "Move! Compel every hand to my ready. Quick now! Quick!"

"Show a leg, m-men!" the terror-bearer screamed. "Atop with ya all! C-c-captain's orders!"

Groans and threats toward the young scout filled the soggy walls as he roused weary wayfarers from their promised and precious sleep. At sixes and sevens, and all but rioting, they floundered out of their berths and up to the overburdened deck.

"Or' yonder, mates!" The skipper aimed the small end of his scope toward the evil armada: two sloops flying black, two flying bloody, and the big ship waving the Chief Thief's Jolly Roger. "Raiders!"

"Oh, God of heaven." A deckhand made the sign of the cross. "Have mercy on us all!"

"Sink me now!" a sailor hollered. "That's Beard! The scourge of the sea!"

"Fish in a barrel, me hearties! No way out."

Kaboom! The thunderous blast, trailed by a shrill whistle overhead, instantly silenced the bleating. The warning shot, fired by one of the approaching sloops, demanded the captain's action.

"Will you fight, men?" The commander challenged his scrambling crew as he white-knuckled the leather handle of his sword. "Will you defend the *Caesar*?"

"They're not soldiers, sir. These are barbarians and cutthroats!"

"We fight, we die, sir. We're outmanned and outweighed!"

He knew his ship and crew were trapped. His best move was to surrender and plead for their lives.

"Strike the colors and to the longboats!" he assented.

The pirates permitted Captain William Wyer and his men to abandon ship and go ashore. They watched as Blackbeard's thugs boarded the *Caesar* and claimed all of the crew's possessions and any objects of value as booty. On April 12, 1718, they looked on as their ship, with its manifest and valuable timber, burned to ashes before their eyes.

This is one vessel of hundreds that Blackbeard's men plundered and destroyed. Plenty were captured, refit, and renamed by the barbarian brotherhood. Many seamen were not as fortunate as the crew of the *Protestant Caesar*.

Blackbeard had captured and cleared the decks with a single shot over the bow. This extraordinary result was owing to the forbidding features of his face, his frame, and his fame—and to the magnitude of his flagship, the *Queen Anne's Revenge*.

Queen Anne's Revenge

"That one, lads, is a prize worth havin'!"

"Aye, Cap'm, without question—a handsome vessel."

"Full sails now, Mr. Hands. We take her before nightfall!"

There are two piratical options in seizing a *prize*: by gentle persuasion or with brute force. Blackbeard proved proficient in both. After a long chase, his cannon-laden sloops caught up with the *La Concorde*, a French slaver from Saint-Malo. Just off the island of Martinique, he went with the latter approach.

"Let fly and prepare cannons; a full complement now!" squalled the Admiral of the Black.

"Fire as you please!" The quartermaster discharged the frenzied fighters, augmenting the chaos and stuffing the air with terror and sulfur.

Surprised by the slightest resistance, Blackbeard shouted to his helmsman, "Bring her alongside, Lord Hands! Ready us to board! We give no quarter!"

With guns blazing and cannons firing, through blinding fog of smoke and ash, the infamous pirate and his seeming innumerable demons besieged the weakened vessel. Steel on steel, hands to throats, swinging on ropes with daggers between their teeth, the intruders forced their way onto the French slave ship.

Pierre Dosset, the captain of the commandeered ship, had allowed his full-rigged frigate and exhausted crew to sail into vulnerable waters and would now pay the price.

Like an army of ants hurriedly smothering a fallen scrap of cheese, the pirates swarmed their prey. Reduced by fatalities and weakened by disease, the sailors of the Guineaman were quickly overwhelmed.

The *La Concorde* was never intended to become a pirate ship. It wasn't meant to be used as a slaver, either, for that matter. Simply put, like many lives, the valuable vessel was captured and refitted to function as an instrument its architects would never have envisioned.

The original purpose of the two-hundred-ton boat, built in 1710, was as a merchantman, designed to carry cargo and passengers. Soon after its maiden voyage, it fell into the baneful hands of French slave traders and accordingly underwent her first refitting. The *Concorde*, which ironically, translated into English, means *peace and harmony with humanity*, was renamed the *La Concorde de Nantes* and went on to demonstrate the exact opposite.

Blackbeard thrived at cultivating an atmosphere of war. Ardently looking for names to shame and lives to ruin, he and his bloodthirsty bullies succeeded in vandalizing any ship within their reach. They were especially hepped up when they could overtake a slave ship because of the particular piratical characteristics of these boats: size, speed, and open spaces for fighting and hauling loot.

Like the money-grubbing slave merchants, when Teach laid eyes on the rough-hewn barracoons, he knew this ship would serve his caustic cause perfectly. According to the Royal Navy, when Blackbeard polished off his renovations, refitted, and renamed it, the *QAR* was a fifth-rate warship. A battle-ready floating fortress with forty cannons and between four hundred and five hundred ferocious felons; she was a vessel of intimidation and destruction.

On November 28, 1717, as nightfall and doom fell upon the *La Concorde*, the Sea Robber likely carried out several pirate practices in his takeover. Each step, a phase in the process of fulfilling a much higher objective. These strategies precisely mirror those of the *Piratas Originalis* as he commandeers people's lives for his purposes and pleasure.

Blackbeard and Beelzebub have the same end in view: hoisting their flag over your ship and declaring to all others, "This one belongs to me and is now under my command!"

Piratas Originalis

They pillage and plunder, rob and rape, terrorize and torture. They destroy lives. They're pirates; it's what they do. Like puppets dangling on strings, these villains are the express image of the Primordial Pirate, Satan.

Jesus repeatedly warns humankind that the overarching obsession of Lucifer, His and your foremost enemy, is to steal, kill, and destroy.

Strikingly, just as Hollywood's version of piratical history has romanticized and satirized the operations and objectives of Marauders, Tinseltown has successfully rescripted our bent on Beelzebub, as well. He's famous these days for being helpful, sensitive, compassionate, even.

As I write, *Lucifer*, a television series, airs on Fox and follows "the original fallen angel, who has become dissatisfied with his life in hell. After abandoning his throne and retiring to Los Angeles, Lucifer indulges in his favorite things (women, wine and song)—until a murder takes place outside of his upscale nightclub." It's in its third season with above-average ratings.

Equally fascinating, though Fox is discontinuing the show, is a #SaveLucifer campaign that persuaded Netflix to pick it up and stream Season 4.

Far beyond the shores of harmless entertainment, this devilishly handsome nightclub owner enlightens his audience that his father, God, is selfish, manipulative, and cruel and that he, Lucifer Morningstar, "never ever lies."

Well, that's a lie. God's Word exposes him: "When he lies, he speaks what is natural to him, for he is a liar and the father of lies and half-truths." (John 8:44, Amplified)

Oh, let me clear up one other thing: In hell, Satan does not have and *never will have* a throne. He's sentenced as a prisoner who will be bound there forever. Some Hollywood fictioneers must have been seduced with John Milton's Luciferian tout: "Better to reign in Hell than to serve in Heaven." No, no reigning will be happening for Satan or any of his hooligans.

But it's not just Hollywood attempting to venomoid the Serpent. *Luciferian* "is a belief system that venerates the essential characteristics that are affixed to Lucifer. The tradition, influenced by Gnosticism, usually reveres Lucifer not as the devil, but as a liberator, a guardian or guiding spirit, or even the true god as opposed to Jehovah."[3]

This is the proven pirate practice called "flyin' a friendly." It's a wildly successful charade ... as you will see.

The Rolling Stones entreat us to have "Sympathy for the Devil." Metallica invites us to cut a rug with him, while Van Halen suggests that keeping pace in this world is only possible by "Runnin' with the Devil." Then there's the legend of the Clarksdale, Mississippi, crossroads.

Robert Leroy Johnson, a young musician ambitiously craving success, "made a deal with the devil." Following the explicit instructions of a superior guitarist, Johnson waited compliantly for a moonless night.

At midnight, he arrived at the intersection near the Dockery Plantation on the Sunflower River between Ruleville and Cleveland, Mississippi.

He handed over his guitar to the Devil, who, in dense darkness—a more powerful dark because of the lack of moonbeams—proceeded to tune it. Before returning the instrument, with its now Satanic strings attached, the Fallen Tunesmith couldn't resist picking a few fiery glissandos.

Trembling with fear and exhilaration, the hands eventually belonging to the king of the Delta Blues gripped the Gibson around the neck as the devil gripped his.

This fatigued Faustian fable has stoked false hopes in many an aspiring artist. The desiring but doubting among us don't need Lucifer to empower us to create supernatural riffs. Though desperate to matter, many concede to a similar pact with him, not so formal but indeed as formidable.

Satan isn't just a thug or a bully. Jesus called him out: "From the very beginning, he was a murderer" (John 8:43). He's not to be trifled with as though he's impotent or some kind of incompetent bumbler. He's an experienced thief, a master manipulator, and the undiluted spirit of murder. He's devoted to devouring any resemblance of life, love, or divine value. This Prince of Darkness is the chief pirate on the high seas of humanity. He's looking for every opportunity to steal, kill, and destroy. At the very least, like a claw-clenching lion, he aches for access to your life.

Like the *La Concorde*, though created for a noble purpose, I've not always sailed according to my divine manifest. I granted the Chief Thief access to my ship. He took the helm and refitted and renamed my life for his destructive use. Only by the grace of God am I alive to tell the tale!

Has Jesus Christ recovered your life from the hold of the old sea dog? Then let my story be an echo of how great is our God! I join your own spirited shout of thanks and honor to He alone Who saves!

On the other hand, if you realize pirates are on your ship, the Pirate of Pride, or the Thug of Fear, Worry, Apathy, or Addiction, let my story encourage you. I hope you believe me when I tell you what Jesus Christ did for me, He can and will do for anyone who will trust Him!

With courage and grace, let's get underway!

THE FALL

"He's definitely dead."

"Oh, my Lord, in heaven!"

"What happened? Did he ..."

"Is he breathing? That was the most horrible thing I've ever ..."

"This is bad! Really bad."

"He fell!"

"He fell? From where? Up there?!"

"Oh, my God! That's, that's gotta be ... ten, fifteen feet!"

"No, from up there! From the top!"

"From ... the ... top?"

"Oh, Lord. That's gotta be twenty feet. He's probably dead."

"Are those teeth? Are those his teeth?"

I smell the coffee.

I don't recognize the muffled noises. Voices maybe. Distant, like when you bob up from the bottom and sink back down again.

Where am I?

Everything is exceptionally dark and cold. I imagine I'm lying on freezing metal.

Like the dog who can't catch his tail, my mind is gasping for a shred of information.

Blinding sharp pain somewhere in my lower back or legs; it's gone as suddenly as it came.

I can't feel or move anything.

I will my eyes to open. Only one obeys, cracking less than halfway. Through lashes caked with gunk, I'm able to make out the tops of muddy shoes and unlaced boots surrounding me that haven't yet given up the melting ice from their early morning duties.

11

I realize now I'm strewn on a concrete floor.

I'm startled by the uninvited attention being given to me by two men in navy-blue suits.

Why are you so close to me?

Overpowering nausea.

The exceptionally tall one folds his way down and pinches my left wrist.

I try to move away. No part of my body responds.

"Can you hear me?" he asks with a lowered but panicked voice.

"Do you feel this?" Pressing, he peers into my open eye for any clue.

Yes, I hear you.

I can't move the words from my mind to my mouth.

Is the floor sliding? Rolling?

Can't ... pin ... it ... down.

Fear erupts in my soul, shallowing up what little breath I have.

Am I dying? I'm so not ready to die.

The heavy emotional-physical fusion of cresting tears is rising in my chest.

Not the pleasureful aroma of fresh brew but the stench of burnt, forgotten coffee on the brink of morphing into tar, like the acrid reek of a blown ballast.

The sweat beginning in the back of my throat, competing with the stone-cold floor, becomes too much to manage.

The low, unyielding drone of the warehouse heaters contributes to my numbness.

I'm going to be sick.

Attesting to being alive, I vomit through the malaise of severe nausea and dizziness. Because I can't move, the spew gets caught in my throat, choking me, presenting a pseudo-convulsion.

"He's having a seizure!"

"Oh, thank God, he's even alive!"

"Somebody grab his tongue!"

"He's okay. He's okay" is whispered vacuously from the crowd, half statement, half question, ringing with collective doubt.

The other man in blue, a cross made with a couple of rusted penny nails swinging from his neck, tries to wipe my mouth with his towel. It reeks horribly of machine oil or Brasso.

"Tell me your name," he says quietly.

Not getting an answer, he tries to reach a different part of my brain.

"Do ya know where ya are?" His Texas drawl comforts me. "What's the date today?"

I have no access to facts.

My browser is taking way too long to load. Just the endlessly spinning wheel.

Abruptly, the feeling of a knife piercing the top of my head shoots liquid fire to my extremities. I feel the blush but still can't budge.

Shock, pain, confusion, all fighting to be tended to.

I can't think of one name, not anyone's—not even my own.

Like a bowl of glass marbles spilled onto the hard floor, my thoughts are sporadic and bouncing everywhere. I can't land one of them.

I try to lift my head. I can't so much as get my face off the steely floor.

I assume I'm lying in a puddle of blood, the unfamiliar but unmistakable taste of thick, salty metal, like syrup, flooding my mouth.

"He can't talk!" someone hollers.

"It's a miracle he's even alive," another affirms, venturing to cast some measure of hope onto the spectacle.

Miss Ruth, one of my warehouse employees, old enough to be my grandmother, stoops down to confirm I am to remain among the living. Gathering her coat about her shoulders and neck, as though she's about to encounter something even more chilling than the ice outside, she lowers her face next to mine. With pursed lips drawn to the side and with squinty gray eyes, she acknowledges the smell of liquor on my breath.

Drawing back, and with a dramatically long and sapient sigh, she slowly wags her head back and forth a few times before she speaks.

"Poor boy," she woefully admits. "Poor" is pitched higher and twice as long as "boy," a tone of sympathy mixed with suspicion. I feel nothing as she maternally touches the wrist the man in blue prodded.

My right wrist, along with my entire arm, is buried beneath my body.

Most of the sweet folks hedging me in believe this is the worst accident they've ever seen. But for Miss Ruth and Mrs. Hixon, and a handful of others, it's a confirmation, the predictable outcome of the choices I've made.

I feel the Stepford-ish nod of the delegation who've known from the beginning this kid will not die a natural death. This is the predicted way the life of an eighteen-year-old boy with a drug and alcohol problem comes to its end.

At this instant, I realize I'm seen for what I am.

I'm thoroughly embarrassed.

I want to get up and run away, as fast as I can.

I can't move.

I'm mortified.

Oh, God! What have I done with my life?

Of the two women, whom I affectionately call "angels on my shoulders," Miss Ruth is the most worrisome, ceaselessly making a fuss over how skinny my brother Ken is and how tired I always look. (Ken lived and worked with me in San Angelo, Texas, for a brief time.) With chocolate pie on a family plate, sealed with Easter-themed cellophane, vegetable soup, and gentle affirmations, she's won my heart.

"Mr. Art"—she would often insist, because I am her boss, on addressing me as "Mr."—"I'm praying for you. I wish you wouldn't use those drugs like you do." She would take my hand, smiling and looking into my eyes. "I'm afraid that you're going to get hurt someday. Or somebody else … maybe hurt somebody else, you know?"

"You better getcher hand outta that fire!" Mrs. Hixon, who is raising several of her grandkids, is more tan-yer-hide-if-I-could in her affirmations.

Knowing I'd show up at the warehouse stoned or hungover, she'd lie in wait for me.

"God won't be mocked, now, Mr. Art!" she'd warn, wagging her teach-you-a-lesson finger at me. "Don't believe that for a minute. He loves you too much for that."

"Yes, I'm sure He does," I'd rebuff with a smile. I would hang on to the "God loves you" part, said in her gravelly voice, to hear it again and again when I was alone. 14

A professing non-hugger, Mrs. Hixon has always made an exception for me. Her hugs are a bit like hugging a barbed fence post. I cherish her effort.

Over and over again, these two saintly ladies have graciously pleaded with me, as though I was one of their own. They've watched. They've warned. They've wondered. Now, here they stand, fussing over someone they've failed to catch in their kindness. I feel their loss.

"Don't try to move, now," orders the rangy man in blue, still on his knees, hunched over me. "We're gonna lift you onto this stretcher."

As he measures my breathing, his face is awkwardly close to mine. I notice the blue and red web of veins in his bloodshot and searching eyes. Tilting to mumble into his shoulder mic, he holds his side-eyed stare on my bruised and bleeding head, just above my open eye.

Someone, or something, holds a vicious, yanking grip on the nape of my neck and another somewhere around the small of my back. I fight against its pull.

I have no leverage, nothing to push back against.

The monotone report of the EMT, in medical or technical jargon I don't understand, fades to a distorted echo as I yield, folding into the cold darkness.

"Bless your heart. You sure must have a lot of people prayin' for ya," the cross-bearing man in blue offers as the only sound reason I'm still alive.

I've yet to find the crucial connection between my thoughts and my tongue.

I wish I could say something.

I have questions and concerns, lots of questions.

My will, the inward part of me that boasts the helm, has lost its grip on my life.

My will has lost the wheel.

It's not up to me now.

I'm not choosing to live, but I'm hoping I will.

Frames of light and darkness are pulsing in a steady rhythm across the ceiling of the ambulance as we pass under the streetlights, still aglow. I imagine I'm lying under a bridge as the train is rolling over my head, sunlight breaking through the craggy planks of the track. My stare is fixed by the spongy but rigid brace they've put on my shoulders and neck.

I see no faces now, only hands darting around my eyes and nose, fixing this, turning that, cleaning here, testing everything. Maybe the blaring, unfriendly, haunting siren I dream I hear is sounding for someone else in someplace else.

"We can't have you lookin' like this, now." His slow Texas style soothes my soul in some familiar way. It matters to him that all of the yuck is cleaned off of my face before they wheel me into the Emergency Room. I'm thankful for his kindness and care, his humanity.

With a scrunched and focused face, he's mercifully mindful to not contribute any further, if possible, to my pain. He's blotting blood, but mostly, he's scraping the crusted puke I've been lying in for the last while that's all but sealed my eye and ear closed.

"Still don't know anything? Can'tcha feel anything?" He prods. "I'll bet you really thought your number was up, huh?"

I can hear his gentle smile as he continues wiping my face with the tender treatment of a medic to a wounded soldier.

"God is good. God is good," he tells me as though he's reminding himself, too. His declaration is as natural as the rhythm of his breathing. With a brief sense of safety, I give in to the lure of lull.

I won't remember what happened for several hours. I won't understand how I got here, to the brink of things, for years to come. Under the weight of dread, pain, and paralysis, reality is fighting to wriggle its way back into my brain.

Like rocks breaking through darkened glass, one at a time, bursts of recall crash into my mind. As each memory reconnects to my soul, I can't resist the assault of guilt and shame.

You deserve this, boy. I've condemned myself.

For the first time since the fall, I feel the warmth of tears trickling down my temples and running into my ears.

Suddenly, a voracious attack from the inside, a solid Sunday punch out of nowhere. I shudder as I remember and rehearse the minacious threat the Pirate had exacted just days before: "I'm going to kill you!"

Sometime after the Chief Thief hijacked my ship and burned my manifest, I plunged into the depths of harsh self-judgment. I don't know if it was the Sultan of Spin dogging me, dragging me, or my own conscience guilting me to the point of deep and crippling harm.

As early as I can remember, there's no one who's ever been tougher on me than myself. But when the Deceiver manipulated his murderous hands onto the helm of my destiny, all of my self-confidence and genuine purpose was strangled. In their place was anchored severe self-contempt and constant culpability. Matter of fact, any trouble around? Mine, yours, or otherwise, I believed it was my fault until proven otherwise. This wasn't self-pity. No, that would have been a step up. This was self-loathing.

How did this happen, you ask?

In my mind and heart, I was raised by the best. I couldn't have been given better parents, siblings, coaches, or teachers. As a kid, I was encircled with love and care, and a divine value was placed on my life. I loved my life and almost everything about it. Until I didn't.

When did I begin to measure the value of my life according to my present situation, condition, or social status? Why was I so profoundly addicted to pleasing other people rather than following my God-given dreams?

How did it happen? How did I, so treasured and enriched by those who loved me, become a weapon of destruction in the plans of the pirate?

I mean, after all, if the pirate had had his way, I would have never been born. Let me show you what I mean.

PIRATES IN THE SHADOWS

Long before the ship's captain is aware of the presence of pirates, options have been weighed and decisions made about him and his vessel. Skilled tacticians of espionage, the Sea Spies follow their prey for days, maybe weeks, gathering critical intel from the shadows. Is the ship alone? Is it strong or weak? Is it armed? Is it carrying valuable cargo? If the robbers consider the prize worth capturing, the only decision left for them to make is will they take it by force or with friendly persuasion.

"If I die, I die. But this child will be born and do the will of God!"

Darting worrisome glances at each other, able to look into her eyes only for a moment, the surrounding panel of medical professionals knew she meant it.

The first pirate attack threatening my destiny happened before I was born. My mother had been warned by her doctors not to have any children. I'm her third. Her pregnancy with me proved the legitimacy of her many physicians' concerns. Throughout her entire pregnancy, she adjusted to sleeping in an upright position because she couldn't breathe while lying down. By her third trimester, she was restricted to bed rest and endured constant medical oversight.

Hunkered around an imposing table in the center of a small, drab, airless room, seven physicians encircled her to make one last attempt to convince her to follow their fears. Perhaps they assumed if they could get enough doctors in the room, all at one time, they'd finally be able to persuade her.

"You must terminate this pregnancy immediately. If you don't, you and your child may die."

Her courageous decision proved to reflect a profound understanding of what she discerned was happening: the Prince of Pirates was making a grand effort to board her ship. My life and destiny would have been lost had my mother allowed her flag of faith to come down.

I'm immensely grateful she held her ground. I'm alive because of the value she placed on my life, her love for God, and her trust in His strength and faithfulness.

This was the pirate's first attempt on *my* life. But know this: as an edgy criminal on the skids who knows his time is short, the Chief Thief is terrified of you discovering God's design and dream for *your* life! He lives in a constant state of panic and will do anything within his reach to abort the plans and purposes your Creator holds in His heart for you.

Awkward and Shy ... and Terrified

I was shy, awkward, and didn't understand the economy of adolescents. Though my family didn't have much money, what I *did* have was a speech problem—I had what the professionals called "lazy tongue syndrome"—a bad haircut, and a horrible complexion. All of my growing-up years, I had to wear hand-me-downs—my sister's! All of this wreaked havoc on my self-confidence. Add to that, I was a scared kid.

I wasn't exactly one of those scared-of-his-own-shadow kids, but close. One of my earliest fear-filled memories was incessantly checking in the bathroom mirror to make sure I still had my eyeballs!

I had ignorantly watched the movie called *The Omega Man* with Charlton Heston. For years afterward, before I could sleep in my own bedroom, I would check in the closet, under the bed, and behind the curtains for any hiding Nocturnals. (Those were the creepy creatures from "the Family" who were shadowing the Omega Man!) As cheesy as it was, in my tender soul, these eyeball-less night monsters—who would steal your eyes if you looked at them—could exist. And if they did, I was convinced I was their next victim.

It didn't help that my brother, Ken, knew how to roll his eyeballs up into his head and out of sight, without using his fingers. Oh, my goodness. Once he experienced my arm-flailing, cookie-throwing, blood-curdling reactions to this devilish device, he was hooked. He invented ways to scare me. Through the years, his plans of attacks became highly developed, if not perfected.

I was afraid of a lot of things: the dark, girls, failure, rejection. What induced the heaviest drape of dread over my soul was a foreboding sense that I would never make the grade. I subsisted under the all-prevailing impression that I'd never measure up to what everyone expected of me, of what God expected of me.

I suppose I felt I was a disappointment to everyone else because I was so displeased with myself. I struggled to make up for my self-perceived defects and self-imposed deficiencies and for what I would later learn to be glaring, but not uncommon, dysfunctions.

In my efforts, I became a perfectionist of which, perhaps you've heard, is the voice of the driven. I was a perfectionist before I even knew what one was. I was cutting and letting myself down at every turn.

"Why are you so stupid?" I berated myself after stuttering my words.

You're worthless, just worthless! would echo in my head, loud and long, from my perceived failures at the most insignificant things.

Soul Crushing

During an early morning science lab class at Chemawa Middle School, in Riverside, California, I was slumped, chin in hand, gazing out through the dirty window, dreaming I was anywhere else but there.

"Arthur? Mr. Evans?"

I heard my name being spoken so faintly I had to decide if it was real. Abruptly, like the thin, monotone voice of the transistor radio suddenly landing on a stereo signal, I heard, loud and clear, "Arthur! Where are you?!"

Mr. Rosen had been repeatedly calling my name, engaging everyone's attention but mine. When it reached my mind that it was me he was shouting at, I was startled.

Bwaaump!

I turned so sharply in my wooden chair it blasted the sound, with comparable volume, of a foghorn as it scooched across the floor! This wake-the-dead detonation signaled my fellow thirty-five classmates to become so quiet the drop of a pin would have reverberated. I was horrified.

With a hollow stare and a kind of irritated smile, when only the corners of the mouth go up, my teacher stood, holding out a piece of chalk as a summons for me to come to the chalkboard at the front of the classroom.

All of the blood, along with any residue of courage, drained from my head and went straight out of my feet. It didn't matter that I had no idea what the present scientific discussion was about. I was too terrified to talk and too petrified to walk.

To make matters worse, once I finally found the fortitude to break what seemed to be an eternal trance of silent fear, I stood up. As I began the painful journey forward, my pigeon-toed feet were tangled in my chair. Straight off of the illustrated pages of the well-worn textbook *How to be a Teenage Idiot*, I went smack-dab to the floor.

Ku-thud! The class flooded with delight and roared with laughter. I never made it to the chalkboard. It's a funny story now. At the time, it was soul crushing.

I don't know if any fourteen-year-old could laugh off the embarrassment of falling and sprawling in front of his or her peers. For me, and for the sharks circling my ship, it was blood in the water.

The Marauder readily discerned that I, like many insecure kids, was alone, awkward, and naive. Callow, like how you feel the first time you attempt to walk across one of those high wooden beams in a ropes course at camp. Approaching it with such confidence and thinking it a manageable challenge, only to be surprised that it's so different, so unfamiliar, so precarious.

When I was alone, I was afraid. When I was with others, I was mostly agitated and anxious. In time, those in the know diagnosed me with ADHD (attention-deficit/hyperactivity disorder). My mind and emotions raced fiercely beyond the boundaries of my control. I've heard ADHD described as "having a race car brain with bicycle brakes." Agreed.

I've often felt as though I'm holding a hundred live wires with only one or two power sockets available. My insecurities, apprehensions, and a burgeoning bundle of disorders measurably molded my outlook on the world and my place in it.

Add to that my lack of confidence and the inability to put two thoughts or words together, and you can understand why I was extremely vulnerable to rejection. I was the kid so uncomfortable in my own skin that I made everyone else around me uneasy as well.

No doubt, by now, dear reader, you're feeling a bit sorry for me. But don't for a moment believe this is my sole experience. We all, in some way or another, fall prey to the fragile self-image and societal pressures placed on our disabilities, deficiencies, and dysfunctions.

For me, these were bits of intel informing the pirates lurking in the shadows that my ship was in the water without friends, without direction—searching. I was desperately wandering and wondering if I would ever find a place in the world where I fit.

"Don't take yourself so seriously!"

There were plenty of other impediments daily threatening my all-important pre-shaven, pre-driving social standing. For example, the loving guardianship of my older sister, Jenna Coy.

Brave and strong, Jenna Coy, whom we've affectionately called J. C. for as long as I can remember, wouldn't take much foolishness from anybody. She, heart and soul—I mean basso-profundo, deep-growl-with-accompanying-snarl heart and soul—could not tolerate the attitude or brutality of bullies.

It seemed like within minutes of our family moving into a new neighborhood, it was fully understood by everyone that a new marshal was in town. The weak and vulnerable were now off-limits to the abusers, whom she forthrightly referred to as *twerps!*

Her care and custody for my friends and me didn't always work in my favor the way she hoped it would. Like the early summer morning when she handed out numbers on a couple of bullies harassing my buddy Olly and me.

We were tossing a baseball in our front yard when our hood's hoodlums, Larry and Charlie, arrived at the brilliant idea of making a game out of guessing how many of our teeth they could knock out with one punch. Their razzing reached J. C.'s ears and "last nerve." (Her words.) With the stature and the stance of nothing less than Wonder Woman, she made her protective presence known.

"Hey! Twerps! You come back into my yard and I'm gonna knock your heads together!"

They hightailed it. For a minute. We resumed our game of catch. But like how a piece of bologna drives a meat-crazed dog dizzy, tyrants can't resist the vulnerabilities of those weaker than them. They came back all the more puffed up to overawe us with their enormous size and toughness.

They may have survived the coming humiliation had they kept their taunts beyond the borders of our yard. I caught a glimpse of Olly's gleeful face and flashing eyes, attesting to the confidence he held in my big sister's word.

SPLAM!

The wooden screen on our front door blasted open and crashed against the side of the house like the ringing of the bell at the start of round one!

Seeing red, J. C. exploded into the yard and on the fly targeted her aim to take care of business. Furious at the audacity of our agitators, who had now challenged her warning, her purposeful you've-crossed-my-line strides and unflinching glare introduced a frightening level of courage apparently foreign to the wannabe thugs.

With gaping mouths and eyes as broad as plates, Olly and I marveled at the spectacular display of power and proficiency. *Someday ... we dreamt ... someday.*

Grabbing a handful of red hair in one hand and a clump of blond in the other, J. C. went right on to knock their heads together. Like thumping a coconut with your knuckles, the hollow *plonk!* as their knuckleheads collided shook us from our enraptured delight.

As quickly as they could find their senses and get their feet under themselves, bully number one and bully number two, squealing like bruised hyenas, scurried down the street, heads in hands until they disappeared from view.

J. C. proved stronger than the biggest and baddest of all the bullies in my world. She saved my hide, if not my life, more times than I can remember. But when the whole school and surrounding neighborhoods knew I was push-around proof because of my big sister's protection, my social status suffered a swift, and anything but silent, death. She meant well.

Then there was Ken, my older brother. More precisely, I'm Ken's little brother. Handsome, smart, witty, and, at least in my estimation, the embodiment of charming by the time he was fifteen years old. *Ugh!*

He was like the Crown Prince of Riposte. He had a ceaseless cache of relevant info about anything and everything. He'd read *Encyclopedia Britannica*, from A to Z, any topic, for the sheer enjoyment of learning—I barely read comic books—and he usually had two good comrades and a steady girlfriend.

I've often thought Ken was kind of Watson-ish. He could be firmly and unequivocally counted on for the perfect quote, joke, pun, or urban legend at any given moment and for any occasion. He would have bankrupted *Jeopardy!*

As Lil Evans, as I was called by my sister's and brother's friends, I was the middle rider in the back seat on family outings, left behind for any events that didn't include at least one of my parents, and was always the last to realize the joke everyone was laughing at was usually on me.

Until I was thirteen, J. C. and Ken had me convinced I was likely adopted and they had no idea who or where my real parents were. I suspect they had heard some rumor that the baby of the family is always spoiled. They weren't going to have any part of it.

"You see how curly my hair is?" Ken pointed out.

"Yeah?" I slowly raised my hand to feel my straight-as-straw hair.

"Well, you know how curly and wavy dad's hair is?" he explained. "That's because he's my dad. If he were your dad, you'd have curly hair, too."

I worried about it for a long time. For quite a while, I strained in the mirror to find a curl or the slightest wave in my hair to which I could hitch my assurance.

Though their nicknames, pranking, and overall normal sibling treatment of me eventually helped to shape who I am today, at the time, I didn't navigate it very well.

If I heard my dad say it once, I heard him tell me a thousand times: "Don't take them or yourself so seriously."

"Just be yourself!"

One evening, as we were clearing the dinner dishes from the table, my dad obliviously detonated the worst possible piece of advice he could have lobbed at me.

I had mentioned how much I admired this guy who lived in our neighborhood. Our whole family knew him. I'd commented on how I liked his style and maybe should wear my hair like he wore his. It was a lot longer than mine, and I was aiming to bring my dad around to the idea that it was okay for boys to have long hair.

"You just need to be yourself," he urged with parental sincerity.

Neither he nor I could adequately explain what happened next. Unbeknownst to him and without any warning to me, he triggered some severe teenage turbulence.

Be myself?

Not only did this grenade of guidance make no sense to me at any level, but it also served as a catalyst for clarity, sharpening my realization of my awkward and overall anathemas of adolescence.

What?!

What does that even mean?

Be myself?

I'm awkward. I have a horrible complexion, a bad haircut, a speech impediment, and—AND—I wear my sister's shabby shirts that button on the wrong side! No, thank you!

I slapped my hands to my cheeks.

"How can you say that?" I wailed. "I'm the ugliest person you've ever seen!" I was so unsure of myself I couldn't hear what he was genuinely saying.

"You're definitely the ugliest person *I've* ever seen." In masterful cadence, as if reading from a cue card, J. C., not one to miss an opportunity to help me grow up, never even looked up from her *Ellery Queen Mystery* magazine as she promptly and matter-of-factly agreed. She went to bed that particular night without ice cream.

As the baby of the family, and doubtless one of the most bunglesome kids alive, I tortured myself far more than anyone else ever did. I used an age-old tool called *insignificance by comparison*. In so many ways, my sister and brother were everything I wanted to be: strong, confident, smart, likable—you know, the reasonable desires of most teens.

I would look at them and the genuine joy they brought to others, including to me, and would ask myself, *What am I going to be? What am I going to do?*

By no one's fault but my own, I felt like a straggler.

A Patient Picaroon

With slow and agonizing perseverance, like a fixated and ravenous lion who's on the verge of a pounce, the pirate circled, patiently studying my struggling ship in the dark waters of fear and disappointment. With the strangle of an inward spiral, each encirclement lessened my prospects; my options were whittled down to a peck of choices, becoming more and more restricted.

I wish I hadn't taken myself so seriously. As an unsure and generally irksome teenager, I couldn't find my way to that distant rationale. I was aching for friends. Like a monster from beneath my bed, shadowy feelings of rejection and despair crawled into my mind as I admitted reality one encirclement at a time. I wasn't likable, acceptable, or friend-able.

The inward coward, critique, and counselor we all possess can be meaner than most.

You're an embarrassment to your family. No one cares about you.

I'd have to adopt and adapt to behaviors not in line with my heart or the guiding principles I'd been raised to honor. Of course, it wasn't true, but I was convinced; it was either that or spend my entire life a social outcast.

Gritting my teeth, I winced as I wagged my drooping head. I realized I was losing myself—the real me. I was conceding. I was becoming someone else, someone different than my disappointed self, someone who could get attention and approval. Maybe acceptance.

"This isn't like you at all."

My dad called the trunk of our 1966 Rambler the "turtle hull." So you know I was raised old-school. I was put on restrictions, lost all kinds of privileges, got whoopins', and had my mouth washed out with soap more times than I can remember.

Now, before you rate my folks, let me gratefully assure you, I wouldn't take the entire world with a fence around it in exchange for my upbringing. Without a doubt, among the few factors God has used to keep me alive is my parents' loving discipline of me.

"C'mon, dude! All you gotta do is make sure nobody's coming," Bobby snapped.

I kicked the dirt and scrunched my face with hangdog disapproval. I distinctly sensed the busy and brooding hoodlums watching from the shadows, gathering, deciding.

"Follow me in," he ordered. "Then, just keep on walkin' around and let me know if anybody's comin'. I'll nab the sausage and walk out. You wait a minute, and then you walk out, calmly."

He looked over his shoulder to be sure he had my attention. "Meet me in the canyon. Got it?"

We were fifteen and always hungry. So, Bobby, my barely older—"fifteen-and-a-half and don't you forget it!"—much cooler, and much bigger neighbor, had punched through the pockets of his olive-green-bomber jacket so that from one side to the other the back of his coat was one big pocket.

"Yeah, I got it," I mumbled reluctantly. I wasn't at all confused with what we were about to do. Nonetheless, on account of Bobby's approval being imperative, the option of telling him to forget it had already been choked out.

Why don't you just walk away? you might be wondering.

That idea never even made an appearance.

It was midday, but the family-owned corner market was freshly cold. It was smallish. Pasty yellow fluorescents lit the aged, uneven, and forever-stained once-beige tiles. Odious, if not nauseating, the smell of bleach and soured milk whelmed every aisle.

I put my hands in my pockets and scuttled in. I trailed far behind Bobby so no one would know we were together.

Bobby closed in on his target, a jumbo log of ready-to-eat sausage. I kept walking with my head down, fists clenched in my pockets. Like a frantic drummer boy of the American Revolution, my heart was pounding out messages of warnings and directions to safety. I ignored its efforts the best I could.

A haunting and irksome rendition of Scott Joplin's "The Entertainer" was being piped through the store's worn-out inset speakers. Haunting because it was a version that sounded like an underwound carousel. Irksome because, oft at my request, my dad would play it on our family piano so we kids could dance around and have fun. Now here I was spoiling the homey tune as it became the background track of my crimes.

So far, so good. Clear sailing as I slunk to the other end of the long row of freezers. The only employee I saw was a lanky college-aged guy wearing a Levi's bandana around his neck and pushing an aisle-wide dust broom. When I turned around, Bobby was gone.

Get to the canyon!

I picked up my pace as I landed hard, intentionally, on the old rubber pad that triggered the glass door to open. On my pivot step, heading for the hills, the pirate made his presence known.

"Hey!" I heard the call and hoped against hope he was yelling at someone else.

"Yes, you, young man!" I looked back from beyond the door with a face of confusion as if to ask, *Who are we looking for?*

The fashionably dressed assistant manager didn't flinch.

"You come with me!" He strong-armed me back inside and hauled me to the back of the store, through the hard plastic swinging doors, and into the dank, grungy back room. We wound our way through open crates of overripe produce: unshucked corn, lettuce, bananas, and other stuff that was supposed to be fresh.

Leaning on each other, to the point of melding together, stacked and soggy boxes of soy sauce, crackers, and dish soap lined the narrow and wobbly staircase to the manager's office. It rattled to the verge of collapsing as we tumbled past it.

"Here's the lookout mouse!" He shoved me into the office, slightly larger than a closet.

I landed on Bobby. I wasn't expecting to see him there. I thought he'd escaped to the canyon. With one side of his mouth turned up and his eyebrows raised like question marks, he shot me the look of blame.

What happened?! he mouthed, as though shouting with discernable displeasure, overemphasizing and dragging out every syllable.

At the moment, I couldn't have cared even an enth less about Bobby's approval or disapproval.

I was sickened with grief and fear, on the order of prison time and never seeing my family again. Of course, no kid is going to prison over a sausage, but I'm red-faced to tell you, that's how naive I was. I was imagining my older self in an orange jumper, talking to my mom through a three-inch pane of glass on a visitation phone!

Heaps of stained and torn boxes lined the walls. Piles of papers and stickers smothered every surface in the cramped room. In front of the one-way window, which was the width of the whole wall, there stood a wooden dresser. It looked like it belonged in someone's bedroom. Its drawers were overstuffed with circulars, coupons, and bright yellow grocery tags.

On top of a thick, oval, multicolored braided rug, mostly brown with dirt, Mr. Garcia, the store's owner, had impelled Bobby to empty his pockets: sausages, marshmallows, crunchy breadsticks, a block of sharp cheddar, and two packs of Bubble Yum gum.

"That's quite a take for one trip, doncha think?" He pitched awkwardly close to our faces.

I couldn't tell if it was to be sure we could hear him over the numbing hum of the freezer's compressors or for dramatic effect. Either way, his intentional nearness was painfully uncomfortable.

"You boys are in a lot of trouble!" he informed us.

Oh, wow! I was startled by the plunder, too. I thought we were in for a snack, not a meal or two with dessert thrown in. Bobby intensified his downward squint, pretending to be overly concerned with his overgrown fingernails. He didn't look up.

"Hey, now." Mr. Garcia's expression lightened as though he was let off a hook of some kind when he recognized me. "You're Arthur. Right? You're Reuben's friend?"

"Sir?" I'd never seen him before, so I was taken aback to hear him say my name. "Uh, yes, sir. I am."

"W-who's Reuben?" Bobby asked with hopeful but wary relief.

"Reuben," I chirped, searching the owner's face, trying to decide if this recognition was in my favor or not. "You know him. He's on our baseball team." I put the names together with the only Reuben I knew.

"This … is … his … dad?" I announced with a side glance of hopeful doubt.

"You're both on my Reuben's team?" the storekeeper asked, one eye raised as he considered Bobby's sideburns and mustache, which could have reasonably belonged to a thirty-year-old.

"Yes! Yes, we are!" Bobby gushed smarmily. "We're all very good friends, sir."

Mr. Garcia forcefully reclined. His decrepit swivel chair shrieked in harmony with his dramatic sigh as he clasped his ink-stained hands together, pursed his lips, and squinted his puzzled eyes. He weighed his new dilemma.

After a whole lot of nodding and squinting, alternating his glare between the two incompetent thieves, he arrived at his verdict.

"Here's what we're gonna do, *mis jovenes.*" The tortured faux-leather chair whimpered in relief as he stood quickly and turned his back to us. Looking out of the big window, he could see his entire store below.

"Normally, we wait here for the police to come and take you away." With hands gently clasped behind him, his voice faded in fatigue as he gazed down into his drab market.

His eldest son, the muscle who had wrested me through the store, shuffled his feet and cleared his throat, denoting disapproval. Junior crossed his arms and clenched his teeth in frustration, wagging his furrowed brow. Undoubtedly, this had become routine for the Garcia family.

I framed in my mind the probability that Bobby and I had joined a long list of scoundrels who had done Mr. Garcia wrong. It tore at my heart.

Anticipating what was about to happen, the younger Garcia threw his hands into the air. "Why not, at least, have 'em do some work?!" he petitioned, if not commanded.

"That's just what I was thinking." With revived enthusiasm, Mr. Garcia, like he was drowning and fighting for air, started throwing invoices, folders, and newspapers to the side and off of the buried desk. Eventually, he excavated the filthy phone and lodged it on top of the pile of fusty papers at our feet.

"Call your parents." He fell back into his chair, relieved he had a plan. "Ask them to come and get you. We'll talk when they're here."

"I don't have a dad," Bobby spit out coldly. "And my mom's in a wheelchair. And we don't have a phone." He let all of this out with the cadence of a prizefighter hoping each punch would knock some mercy into his target.

Mr. Garcia sat in silence, entirely unfazed. He lifted his eyes and scrunched his raised chin into a doubtful side-glance as he refocused on Bobby's face.

"What happened to your dad?" Junior wasn't persuaded, either. "Where is he?"

"He died," Bobby explained from a suddenly tempered heart. "He was shot ... on accident ... when I was five." He instinctively dropped his head.

"I'm sorry to hear that, son." Mr. Garcia was contritely affected. "I'll take you home."

"My dad knows his mom," I spoke up. "He's tellin' you the truth. My dad'll take him home."

Both Garcias stood, arms crossed, staring at Bobby as though they couldn't decide whether to be embarrassed for him or themselves.

I made the onerous call.

All the old-school you can imagine was heaped on me that day! Amid all the discipline, the lectures, the tough love, and the months of working for Mr. Garcia every Saturday morning, there was one phrase that punctured my soul.

Long after dark had settled over our part of the world, my dad finally made it back to the car after talking with Bobby's mom. He was lost in humorless thought as he closed the door and started the engine of our 1972 Gran Torino.

Our drive home, eerily shadowed by moonbeams dancing through the burdened branches of the golden rain trees and the dim lights of the dash, was chilled-to-the-bone quiet. At last, a wave of relief intervened as we turned onto our familiar street and, finally, into our driveway.

On the last jerk and jostle of the car settling into park, my father reached and put his right hardworking hand on my just-caught-stealing hand. After a time, long enough for me to wonder if he was going to say anything, looking straightforward as though he was still driving somewhere, he sighed. "This isn't like you at all, Arthur." A deeper sigh. "Not at all."

I sat alone in the moonlit car and watched the shadowy figure of my dad disappearing into the house. I knew he was right. His words lodged in me like a sharp splinter.

Hurting or shaming my family always brought on an ache of sorrow like nothing else. There was nothing to soothe it. Like the manacled captain, pushed down and locked away in the belly of his own ship, my remorse, the heart of the real me, had to be shushed and squelched.

I was being dragged out to sea. I was further from the warm and safe lights of home than ever before.

FINDING A FOOTHOLD

"Flyin' a friendly" is one of the most effective piratical tactics. Upon approach, the robbers hoisted a flag from the home country of their prey. This would disarm the captain and crewwhile their malevolent enemies advanced unchallenged.

As the pirates crept closer and became more visible, the flags I saw flying above their ships weren't the skull and crossbones or the proverbial horns and pitchfork we often assign to the devil. No, these were banners of benevolence and belonging.

"Hey, you're Arthur. Right?"

No one had put two words together in my direction my entire first year of high school. Now, out of nowhere, one of the most popular, well-liked guys in my school initiates a friendship? Not likely. In pirate speak, this stratagem is called "flyin' a friendly."

I generally felt invisible. So, timidly, I looked to the left and to the right, far from confident he was talking to me.

"I've seen you around school a bit, but I didn't know you live so close to me." Zach, an eleventh grader and a distant stranger, spoke so kindly, comfortingly even, as though he'd known me for some time. "There's a party tomorrow night at Sadie Turner's house. You should come with me!"

I was so desperate for acceptance, I never considered the cost of taking his invitation. I let down my guard, thinking I'd finally been given some kind of break. In actuality, I gave the pirates a foothold.

The Soul Hunter ensured that once I could make out his colors, I'd be enticed with his "good intentions." He closed in on my life, flying the friendly flag of help and hope. The terrifying and terrorizing would come later.

Follow Your Heart

I was born on a Thursday and in church the following Sunday. By the time I'd made it to high school and felt the load of navigating my own vessel, I'd had one canon firmly fastened to my ship: *Follow your heart!*

"In the moment of temptation or trouble, Arthur, follow your heart." My dad dutifully dispensed essential breadcrumbs. "It may save your life!"

Oh, how I wish I would have.

Just to show up at this party, I had to lie to my parents and sneak out of my house at an exceptionally late hour. If these death-defying acts weren't enough, I was going to meet up with people I knew didn't like me, and of whom I was positively afraid. All of this in an attempt to gain friends who didn't care about my life, my future, or my destiny.

Thinking back on it, every kid at that party was probably just like me: lonely ships on the endless ocean of life frantically searching for a flag of significance to fly above our precious lives. Good or bad, right or wrong, at some point, we all want to show we believe our colors have value and meaning, that we're worth something.

With the shiny lure dangling in front of me, in my heart, I knew what to do. What I did was something dangerously different: I followed my head.

I made the soul-shearing, destiny-threatening decision to open the door to the pirate, who, as I remember, looked notably smug. He knew I was on the hook. When I searchingly turned back, it seemed as though all of my father's breadcrumbs were gone.

I was your garden-variety babe in the woods, entering into a world of shadows, sounds, and risks I knew nothing about. I was naive and scared. I know now, but I also knew then, I shouldn't have gone to that party.

Relax, the Ol' Sea Dog mollified. *It's just a party. You'll be fine.*

I was bamboozled from the beginning. The pirate's empty promises appealed to me through my starving curiosity and my need for companionship.

In the warm glow of my pre-teen dreamlife, the sight or smell of booze or marijuana had sent me running for the safety of home. With alarms blaring, red lights flashing, and flares bursting high in the sky, I'd been warned from birth about the traps and destructive power of drugs. I distinctly remember, in the innocence of my impressionable mind, resolving I would flat-out never smoke pot or drink alcohol.

But that was before; before I was converted to believing that resisting drugs or abstaining from liquor would all but vaporize my social status.

I was so pinched with a need to be in good with my peers, I morphed. I began living my life as someone other than the true me. The refitting of my ship was underway.

I wish I'd had the courage to fight back against this destructive ploy. My driving desire for acceptance, though, obliterated all other options.

Welcome to the Party

Even though I was one of the biggest freshmen in my school, I walked with an all-subsuming timidity. I was a big kid on the outside and a dewy-eyed kid on the inside. Like so many teens, I felt like my clothes were wrong, my hair wasn't cut right, my face was riddled with acne ... the list of loathing goes on. I was about as comfortable in my body as a wet cat walking on sand. I believed everyone else was clearly better than me and that I was a poser.

Like grappling hooks, tugging and tearing, the pirates twiddled and twisted all of this to trap me in sludge-level self-consciousness, self-questioning, and self-hatred. No matter what I did, my inner critics, my flaw finders, were always right: *You're a pathetic loser! A nobody.*

Stabbed by the darting eyes of the disapproving, my breath ran short, failing to keep up with my racing heart. Chin to chest, my clenched fist drilled deep and gripping into the pockets of my too-small jacket, I was holding on for dear life.

I scuffled under the ill-boding stone archway, housing a tall, elaborately sculpted, wrought iron gate, and into the backyard of the mansion. I confess I was awed just walking into the first entrance of several. The party, along with my nerves, was exploding. Literally.

From the deep end of the empty swimming pool, a feverish rock band was blasting heavy metal music. Creeping up from all sides of the pool was the folding fog of dry ice with some kind of pulsating red lights underneath it.

The smoke of cigarettes and pot, alcohol fumes, and the puffs of carbon dioxide from the fog machine filled the crisp night air with smells that were terrifying to me. Naively, I was sure I'd stepped into the fires of hell! I was far beyond the boundaries of my comprehension and the comforting lights of home. No breadcrumbs in sight.

"My feet are flyin' baby!"

I had edged into a huddle of sniffers. I was transfixed by what I was seeing.

Several in the growing circle held plastic bags, like those you'd peel off the roll in the produce department to put your bell peppers in. Others, smiling all crazy-eyed like vendors at a carnival cotton-candy stand, were shaking cans of various household cleaners, cooking sprays, and hairsprays. One of the poison peddlers was doling out spray-paint. I can still hear the death rattle of the metal pea clacking in rhythm to the shaking of the can while trance-eyed nosers waited for their malignant mist, quite literally breathless.

One after the other, huffers held out their plastic bags to be filled with aerosol. Once filled, like putting on an anti-oxygen mask, they quickly fixed the asphyxiate-filled bag over their noses and mouths and inhaled.

"Slow it down, man!" How-tos were given. "Just breathe. Just let it happen."

I watched as the baggers welcomed the swirling substance into their nasal passages, intentionally overwhelming the cilia, the tiny hairs divinely designed to filter out harmful toxins from the air we breathe before it reaches our lungs, brain, blood, and nervous system. There was nothing normal or natural about the whole thing. As though they'd been spurred with an urge of sadistic destruction, the gassers giggled and nodded approval toward one another as they watched several of their puffing pals exhibit symptoms similar to suffering a stroke or having a seizure.

As if her legs were made of rubber, the kid closest to me passed out and fell down into a kind of heap. Heart in my throat, I bent down to help her up.

"Oh, ho! Lights out, baby, lights out!" Hah! Hah!" one of the guys holding a can of air freshener guffawed as though talking through molasses. "Better let her be."

Following the orders of the heavy-lidded lead lunatic, I buried my common sense and stood to walk away.

Kawhump!

No sooner had I gathered my scattered bearings than another puffer, maybe two or three feet from me, violently convulsed. Choking on the blood flowing out of his nose, his eyeballs rolled back as he blacked out and fell facedown, thankfully onto the grass. I panicked.

I gripped his shoulder and shook him firmly. "Hey! Are you okay?" I put my face close to his trying to detect any response.

He sounded like a clogged vacuum cleaner, thrashing side to side gasping for air. After a few moments, he recovered his wind and his wits and answered my question.

"Back off, man!" he blurted, spitting blood onto my chin and shirt collar. "Leave me alone! This is my high."

He numbly closed his eyes and curled into the fetal position. "Welcome to Oz, baby," he whimpered as blood bubbled in the corners of his mouth.

Like a bull with a ring in his nose, the pirate yanked and jerked my soul with violent confusion and worry. I had no idea how this world worked.

You've got a lot to learn, little boy, he gibed. With the slightest tug of rejection or embarrassment, he turned me whichever way suited and amused him.

"Here ya go!" Sadie, a girl I recognized from school, commanded snidely as she shoved a clear plastic cup of Crown Royal into my hand. "This, dear sir, is your ticket to party with us!"

It was mixed with just enough cola to make it drinkable without completely burning your house down.

She and her huddled court of a few pretty, upperclassmen girls, apparently the governing council of the gathering, glared at me with a look as if to say, *This is no joke! If you want to be here, you'll drink this and anything else we put in front of you.*

Warning flags, flares, and flashing lights, and every other kind of danger signal you can imagine, were flying by at top speed. Aching for acceptance, I deflected every caution. I drank it.

Up to this moment, I had never consumed alcohol, smoked tobacco or weed, or used any kind of drugs. I had no reference, no gauge or meter. I didn't realize my aggressors would likely have been appeased had I only sipped the drink.

I filled my mouth with the jet fuel and gulped quickly.

With teeth and talons, like a lethal mixture of cayenne, turpentine, and horseradish root, the ethanol scorched the skin from my throat and proceeded to rip the back of my head open in one shred!

At once, as if to deny entry, my eyes closed and I doubled over, hurling my head toward the ground, and my nose blew snot and liquor like a gross geyser! My face flushed hot, my eyes filled with tears, and my ears rang with a high-pitched whistle like they'd been sternly boxed.

Intrigued by my convulsive condition, if not entertained, the growing jury of stunned girls stepped back and goggled in peeved wonder. After an eternity passed, through the humming in my ears and the roar of my uncontrollable heaves, I heard the hooting and hollering of the ringleader.

"Oh-uh. My-uh. God-uh!" An eruption of uproarious laughter rose all around me. "That's the most pitiful thing I've ever seen," Sadie said, one hand anchored on her hiked hip, the other waving her glass of whatever—twice the size of the cup she'd given me.

With a spectacular wag of her head, a flit, and a spin, she and her entourage evaporated into the crowd.

You idiot! The heartless henchman, with a sinister coldness reserved for adolescent rejection, sadistically ground my self-image to dust. *You can't do one thing right.*

The worst I could have imagined actually happened. Gobsmacked, I stood shuddering and bewildered in what seemed to be the white heat of every spotlight in the universe.

I've gotta get out of here.

Hurriedly, I lifted my head to look for the gate I'd come in through. I couldn't see farther than two or three feet. The disastrous event had so detonated my insides, along with my eyeballs, I felt like my brains were leaking out through every possible aperture.

The pulsing crowd, shrouded in the thickening fog ascending from the pool, flashing, roving lights, and my own temporary burn and blur all anchored my feet to the floor. I couldn't budge.

He's with Me

"Well, that was embarrassing," a small, raspy voice squeaked from the shadows.

"Small sips. Small sips," the stranger instructed. "You'll be all right."

His voice sounded older, much older, than a kid at the party—maybe forty or fifty.

I didn't want to be *all right*. I wanted to be somewhere else. I wanted to be at my home, safe in the sweetness and sympathy of my mom and dad.

I flinched and whirled to see whose tiny hand had dropped onto my shoulder. What I saw flustered me even further.

At fourteen, I was nearing six feet tall. I assumed someone with a voice sounding as old as he did would be at least as tall as me. When I turned, it took me an extra second or two to find him in the dark.

I saw a grown man, but one much smaller than me and significantly shorter than I was anticipating. He was dressed all in black, from the silver tips of his gaudy boots to the top of the flat cap he was wearing backward.

My neck and head craned downward, straining to see into the darkness. I could barely make out the frame of his face in the glow of his cigarette; the rising smoke added blur to my stinging eyes.

With his chin dipped down and faint brows lifted, he looked at me from the top of his glassy, raddled eyes. The wiry figure jerkily offered his frail hand.

"I'm Andy," he mumbled slowly around his bouncing long-ash cigarette. "Who're you?"

Still recovering, I hesitantly and tensely shook his icy hand. "Arthur." I knew I was out of my depth.

"Well," he continued talking before I finished saying my name, "I've never seen ya at any of our parties. You're new here."

"No, I'm ..."

"Well, no matter." He gazed off in the direction of the chaotic crowd, as, from the inside pocket of his leather jacket, he slowly pulled out what looked like a cowboy's cigarette.

"You gotta slow down on the hooch, man. Ya don't wanna go and get hammered," he exclaimed, as though he was expecting a collective agreement from the flock, who weren't even listening. "Hah! Nobody wants ta see that!"

Hooch? Hammered? I had no idea what he was talking about. I tossed my head back with half a smirk and a sturdy *humph* to prove I was in control.

He swapped cigarettes, lighting the hand-rolled joint with the smoldering stub of his smoke. The initial plume hauntingly masked his face. The sour stench of marijuana sucker-punched me in my gut. What I'd been warned about and admonished to run from, by all of the people in my life who cared about me, was now, in the truest sense, being blown into my face. I could hear heavy boots thudding against the deck as more raiders landed on my ship.

"This is the good stuff here, now!" He assumed I knew what he was talking about. He held out the lambent reefer in front of me in his small trembling hand. I'd learn later, because of a nerve condition, neither his hands or his feet would ever rest.

"Nah, thanks. I don't want any." I shied, turning my head away, hoping that was the end of it. "I gotta go."

As I looked back toward the pool and the clamorous crowd, Sadie, the princess of the party, and all of her pretty pawns were bouncing toward me. Round two.

"Hey, you!" she howled. I almost answered before I realized she wasn't talking to me.

"Ann-dy! You made it!" She bent down and bravely kissed him on his aged and ragged cheek, accompanied by the approving giggles of her court. "I'm so glad you're here."

"Hello, dear," Andy crooned smoothly. "Do you know my friend, Arthur?" He slowly tilted his head and raised his brows toward me, offering the joint to someone in the group encircling us.

"He's with you?" She spun sharply to re-examine me as though she was seeing me for the first time.

"Arthur?" she asked, squinting her flashing eyes in doubt. "That's your name, sweetie?"

I nodded anxiously with half a smile, running my sleeve under my nose still trying to recapture some composure, if not some degree of coolness.

"Why didn't you say so, for heaven's sake?" she hollowly coddled. "Any friend of Andy's is a friend of mine."

Just like that, I was in. A nobody to a somebody. With a wave of the pirate's hand, I, the incompetent bungler, was exalted to rebellion royalty by a complete stranger.

I would soon become a sought-after bagman baron, someone who could be counted on to always have a hefty supply of pot, speed, or cocaine at the ready. What a setup. Any honest pusher will tell you, "You play, you pay."

As the grog diffused its toxins into my brain and blood, a kind of mellowness settled over me. The pirate wasn't trying to help me feel better. He was strategically targeting my vulnerabilities, my needs, with the earnest intention of gaining full access to my life.

Having sized up my life as he shadowed my ship, the human personality specialist knew alcohol was a play-for-keeps foray to use against me. With my racing mind and unmanageable social awkwardness, alcohol armed me with—albeit artificial—calm and courage. As destructive as this vice is, it's no wonder why it's appealing to so many.

There's a reason why booze is called "spirits." It's a cheap jury-rig for the calm and courage resulting from knowing that God is for you and with you. It's a poor substitute, at best. Its relief is temporary and requires you to drink more and more to experience its anticipated effects. Soon, the trip turns tragic.

As it turns out, what you thought you owned owns you. Far too late, reality strikes. Your flight of fancy crash-lands in a heap of hellacious torment. You've opened your life to the seducing power of a tyrant who intends to ruthlessly take control. If I'm describing your life, with this or any other kind of addiction, don't raise the white flag just yet. Read on. There's hope!

I don't know if it was my willingness to go along with the price of popularity: compromise, or if our accord was struck upon our shared-need of a toxic substance to feel good about ourselves and one another. Either way, for the time being, I was approved by the highest court in the land. As far as I was concerned, I couldn't turn back.

My liability, to myself and my captive-counterparts, quickly shifted to an expectation of loyalty to the pirates now governing my ship. I was an utter landlubber on the tides of quid pro quo.

"Let me know when you change your mind," Andy said after the parley had left us. His tone informed me he was fully aware of my indebtedness for his agency in dealing with the hierarchy. "It'll make ya feel a lot better. Calm your nerves. You know."

Not ready to go completely overboard just yet, I twisted my mouth up to one side and shook my head. "Nah. Thanks."

"I'll tell ya what." Andy jutted his chin and urged with heightened interest. "You take this and give it to that guy right there, the one in the yellow jacket, and I'll put some weed in your pocket to take home. You can try it later."

Standing in the palm of his left, tatted, ring-on-every-finger hand, was an aluminum Kodak 35mm film canister.

"Whaddya think?" He studied my face from the top of his eyes.

I regripped the familiar lining of my jacket pockets and rocked on my heels. I arrested the deepest breath I could manage as I deliberated and contemplated.

"What's in …?" I asked.

"Don't you worry 'bout that!" he said. "Something he's paid for. Just put it in his hand and tell 'im it's from Andy."

I delivered Andy's goods to the fellow in yellow, and as promised, the troller sent me home with my first dime of weed (a baggie with enough marijuana for about ten joints). I'd go on, for the next few years, supplying my schoolmates and others with Andy's merchandise. He never paid me in cash but saw to it that my own ruinous habits were always cultivated and ravenous. As long as I was hooked, he had a mule to manage and manipulate.

On the streets and in my soul, my walk home from the party was shadowy. Monsterlike and mystical moonlit trees, cocooned with hanging fog, escorted me at an hour of the night when I should have been safe and sound in my bed. My heart and head were dodging irrepressible images of the party, ratcheting up my guilt and anxiety.

In the distance, I heard a siren and panicked. *Is that for me?* My fear was without the filter of experience. As far as I could imagine, someone had called the police and they were on the way to pick me up.

Drugs? Alcohol? Runaway? I couldn't wrangle my imagination. So, I dropped my head, pulled up my hood, and picked up my pace. A firetruck zoomed by on a distant cross street. I was almost to the top of my street.

Oh no!

I rounded the corner and saw the porchlight of my house breaking through the misty fog.

Why is the light on? Why would anyone still be up?

My mind began to reel in an altogether different direction.

What will I say? Can I sneak in? Do I smell like pot or alcohol? I'm dead.

I was thinking about tapping on my brother's window when my dad opened the front door and stepped out onto our small porch. I stood staring into his pain-filled eyes. My guts churned for dear life. I was about to throw up. So, I gulped trying to keep it all down.

"Where ya comin' from?"

"Wally's house," I answered, looking to the ground at my feet.

"Wally's been here, with Ken, this entire evening," he informed me. "Let's try again. Where have you been, Arthur?"

"I went to a party at Sadie Turner's house," I said, as I clutched the bag of pot in my jacket pocket. "I'm really sorry, Dad. I know I shouldn't have."

"I'm sorry, too, Arthur." I always hated it when my parents apologized to me about some infraction I'd committed. It landed me the double-whammo punch of guilt and sheer terror of the punishment coming.

He stepped closer and rested his firm but tender hand on my shoulder. "I'm sorry you're so unhappy with your life that you need to sneak out, lie, and risk so much."

His eyes filled with tears as he hugged me. "Brush your teeth well before you turn in, and say good night to your mother." Neither was a request. "She's very worried about you."

I slipped off my hood and went into my quiet and peaceful house. I was slightly comforted by the lingering smell of buttery popcorn, an early evening ritual my mom and dad enjoyed.

How could all of this have happened so fast?

Or did it? I remembered the boiling frog my dad had warned me about. "Just turn up the heat a little at a time; he'll never know."

My mother's voice startled me from my vacant stare into the mirror, as I brushed my teeth.

"Arthur? Is that you?"

"Yes, ma'am," I mumbled, spitting hard into the freshly scoured sink. I did what I'd seen on an episode of *Hawaii Five-0*. I cupped my hand over my mouth and nose for a breath test. I couldn't smell a thing. I decided I had no idea what I was doing.

Short of breath and dizzy with angst and dread, all I could think about were the bad decisions I had made, like a row of falling dominoes, one after another. I stole one last condemning glance at my reflection before I trudged down the long, dimly lit hallway to my father and mother's bedroom, hopefully to just say good night to my waiting mother.

"Are you okay?" Leaning back on the headboard of their bed, she looked up at me as she laid her book across her lap. Even in moments of dire stress, my mom is the most composed lady I've ever known. I knew not to mistake her poise for passivity.

"I'm fine," I claimed in my strong I've-got-it-all-together voice.

She smiled and nodded gently, not fooled for an instant.

"What could you have possibly been thinking?"

I pursed my lips and crossed my arms in a huff as I tossed my gaze to the ceiling.

"Okay. How about a question you can answer?" she lovingly urged and patted the bed for me to sit next to her. "What do you think of when you hear the word *destiny*?"

"I don't know," I said, rigidly shrugging my shoulders and wagging my head, refusing to sit down. I was sure she would catch a whiff of what I'd been up to.

"It means that you have a purpose," she said as though I'd never heard her explain it before. "You have a destination to shoot for."

My eyes darted repeatedly toward the door as I wobbled nervously from one foot to the other.

"I want you to look at me now. Listen to what I'm saying."

She wanted to say so much more. Discerning the distance between us, I watched her intentionally pull back. Maybe she was worn with worry. Or maybe, because my attitude and countenance were insolent, she thought there would be a better time to talk.

"Well, let me say this to you, Arthur." She refreshed her posture and took my nail-gnawed hand into hers. "Please remember, as much as God, the One who made you, has a plan and purpose for your life, so does your enemy, the Devil." Firmly holding my eyes with her own, she suspended her words but not her expression, allowing each syllable to reach its target.

Then, as though each word were the weight of a cannonball, she advised, "And he plays for keeps, Arthur. He aims to destroy all that is precious in your life."

I wrenched up one side of my mouth and offered half of a smile, nodding in toleration of this most miserable moment.

"Your dad and I care about you and we pray for you, every day." She let go of my hand and resumed her book as if to graciously relieve my tangible torture.

"Follow your heart, son." She couldn't resist. "It seems to me, you don't know where you're going or how you're going to get there. But I'm convinced you can hear the voice of Jesus in your heart."

"Yes, ma'am," I said, hoping the less I offered, the quicker the encounter would be over.

I wish I could have honestly denied the truth in what she'd said. But too many times, I'd heard and followed God's lead, and He had genuinely helped me. I was just so desperate for friends or, at the least, acceptance. I was willing to do whatever it took.

I'm embarrassed to tell you, while she was sharing such heart-drawn words, all I was thinking about was how to manipulate the situation, even the truth, in my favor.

"Please go to bed now," she ordered.

For a fleeting moment of relief I thought I'd been let off the hook.

"Your dad will deal with you in the morning." I was promptly yanked back into reality.

In those few sacred moments, my head safe on my pillow, in the solitude of my thoughts, over and over, until wearied, I replayed the events of the night. I tried to anchor my soul in a pleasant image, a positive memory. It was difficult.

I had left the party with pats on my back and my name on everyone's lips. I had made the cut. I was in. But I knew they had welcomed an imposter. They had befriended a fake. My jilted soul, cut to the quick, was a raging storm I couldn't calm.

The takeover was well underway. I believed I could measure the foothold I'd opened for the pirate. I thought I could consent to his input but contain his influences. I'd welcomed him on my ship as a friend, someone who had promised to promote me.

Do you remember the TV commercial for Captain Morgan's rum? The charismatic pirate is all smiles, jovial and generous. This is the image of the pirate, leading his singing crew of freebooters as they carouse their way up the plank to board my life. He knew, due to the decisions I had made, that the only One who could protect me could do nothing about his advances. I had exercised my will and opened the door.

He led me to believe I was the one managing things, and he was just coming on for the thrill and morale. We were to have an arrangement, an agreement. He gave his word, and I trusted him. All the while, the Puppet Master was tying on the strings and wires with which he would manipulate my life for years to come.

Exhausted, beat down by shame and leveled by fear, I fell asleep.

My addictions to weed, cocaine, and alcohol grew deeper, forcefully entwined with my dependence on recognition, approval, and acceptance from others. Though my new relationships were as shallow as my pockets, it seemed like, for now, I had a bit of pocket change in the economy of adolescence. I admit, it felt good to not be alone. But, as you already know, acceptance has its price.

Securing a Stronghold

Reflecting on the skill sets of criminals of every generation,
Blackbeard's most mesmerizing trait was his intellect. He had a
persuasive command of words, and an all but supernatural prowess of
reading and manipulating people. Like the Chess Master who plays
from a superior point of view—and sees as many as ten to fifteen moves
ahead—pirate captains mentally mapped every possible reaction their
victims may have in response to their approach or attack,
ready to exploit their prey at every turn.

For many agonizing days after the party, the waters surrounding my ship were ferocious and violent. Daggers of guilt and shame flew at me from deep within my heart. I'd let the plank down to my fraudulent friend. In so doing, I felt I had let God, my parents, and myself down. But so far, I consoled my complaining conscience, this was the better way for me.

I steeped my thoughts in my new feelings of acceptance. I celebrated my courage. I applauded my aptitude. I took account: before the party, no one knew my name. Now, I was at least in the game. I was far beyond my depth, but I was in the game. The pirates were flooding onto my ship. Even in the flux of chaos, condemnation, and complications, it all seemed worth the risk.

I'm not sure how long an imposter is regarded as an imposter before his conduct is considered to be veritable attitudes and actions of the genuine person. It felt as though the pirates and my playacting soul were holding my heart hostage. Promises made and appointments scheduled, I was quickly up to my neck in critical obligations that I couldn't possibly skip out on. As the middleman, I had one hand in my dealer's dope bag and the other in my patron's pockets. Both sides demanded delivery.

Along with my habits, relationships, and attitudes, the pirates altered my daily routines. Before the party, I would walk to school alone or with a fellow nobody. After the party, my morning route to school included a stop-off at Andy's place to pick up dope to be sold or given away per his directions. He required me to come to him each morning because he didn't trust me with more than a buck's worth ($100) of merchandise at a time.

The pirate's hand was in this, too. Regular stops by my dealer's drug house engraved his face, voice, temper, and expectations into my soul. Not only had I been recruited, but in short order, I was drafted into his world and his way of doing things.

Mandatory for success and survival in the flagitious world of drug trafficking, I became the consummate chameleon. Depending upon who I was dealing with, I learned to change my colors—my tone of voice, posture, attitude—as easily and naturally as breathing. Like an actor on a stage, I picked up new roles every day. Timidity gave way to temerity, or, vice versa. I developed superior skills of deception and disguise.

Like a kid who had found the ambrosial candy drawer, my masks worked so well, I frenziedly created more. I compulsively invented a false front for every person in my life. I made a mask I wore for my family and one I put on for my new friends. I even designed one to wear when I was alone to shield me from shame and fear. All the while, the true me was boiling, suppressed below in frustration and aggravation, with deep-seated conviction. I was losing myself and felt powerless to do anything about it. Mask making had become my new mania.

The exasperation of my weakening grip struck me something fierce one day when the gap—between the real me, the person I knew I was in my heart, and the new me, the one cooperating with the pirate and his plans—became insurmountable. Peace was gone, and in its place, rooting deeper and deeper in my soul, was anger and rage.

I Never Saw It Coming

Blood-red face, veins popping, eyes as big as plates, I was beside myself!

It was ten in the morning and the heat index was already at 95 degrees. Summer temps, in Riverside, California, rarely dip below 80 degrees even during the night hours.

Summer league basketball had started, and my team was in the middle of the third hour of a four-hour practice. Outside, on a blacktop court, we were surrounded by concrete and brick buildings and high, rusty chain-link fences. Even our basketball net was made out of chains. No shade was in sight. It was scorching.

Our assistant coach knew we could use the emotional boost of some upbeat music in the furnace. He was a Beatles fan so "Hello, Goodbye" was blasting through his boombox, intended to fuel our play.

Running as point guard for my squad, I dribbled the ball to my right with intention, trying to make it past the defender and open up a play. I dipped my shoulder to turn the corner.

"Not today, boy," he muttered and jutted his knee into my leg. My feet slid on the loose gravel and went up and over my head. My shoulder and head slammed the ground! I skidded on my arm and leg for several feet, leaving a wake of molted skin.

Without thinking, I jumped to my feet, gathered the ball and all the force I could, set a bead on his head, and heaved the missile as hard as possible!

"Hey! You, @#$%^!" I screamed, revving up to rush him. I quickly reconsidered when I realized the whole world had come to a complete halt.

My coaches and teammates were shocked, powerless to continue. I was the most stunned. Practice, music, time all froze. Twenty-seven people, mouths gaping, shoulders protectively raised and locked at their ears, holding their breath with iron-gripped bewilderment, stared at me as though I was a stranger.

I'm thankful and was relieved to report I missed his face. The ball caught just enough of his chin to protect his throat from being walloped. It could have been so much worse.

This knee-jerk reaction was entirely out of character for me. No one, including myself, had ever seen such rage from me. In manic ferocity, I felt like I was watching a scene in a movie of someone else's life. It all happened so fast, so surprisingly. Before my better judgment had the opportunity to weigh in, my rage-driven ego had already erupted. I was no longer at the helm. Bewildered and breathless, I couldn't believe what had happened. I never saw it coming.

"Evans!" my coach thundered. "Not on my team or my time! Four laps and hit the showers." He knew I needed distance from everyone, and that I shouldn't be allowed to continue with the practice.

Pulsating in fury, I gave the best dissolve-you-with-a-death-stare-if-I-could look to the guy who had intentionally knocked my feet out from under me. He had humiliated and embarrassed me. Like sizzling bacon on the hot asphalt, I was livid.

My anger welled up inside of me like an erupting volcano. I wanted to scream or hit someone. Instead, I white-lipped as tight as I could and spit, Clint Eastwood-esque, and left to run my laps seething and teary.

I felt amateurish against the persistent pull of the pirate's systematic takeover. The tug-of-war between my heart and my head was intensifying like the rhythm of my running.

I heard somewhere, if you ever find yourself caught in a pit of quicksand, don't panic and don't fight. Relax and wait for help. The more you fight, the quicker you sink into the bottomless mire. I was wrestling with all my might and plunging faster than I could rationalize.

Toward the end of my laps, I ran out of my red mist and directly into the silt of sorrow for what I'd done. I had hurt someone without even thinking about it. I felt it way down in my bones: my soul was not only being manipulated but mutated. I was evolving, transforming into a different person. I had forfeited my footing, my focus, and my faith and didn't know what to do about it.

Soul vs. Spirit

Please don't misassign blame. Remember, the pirate and his band of tyrants could not have come onto my ship without my consent. In my desperate need for acceptance and approval, I had let down my guard, opened the door, and offered him a foothold. As you can expect of all pirates, he wasn't nearly satisfied to just be on board.

He'll do all he can to maximize his mileage out of our weaknesses and ignorance and drive us as far away from God's presence and plans as he possibly can. He wants to red-pencil your Creator's story for your life and rewrite you for his own purposes and pleasure. He can do none of this without your cooperation.

Charles H. Spurgeon said, "A man is not saved against his will." I would add:

> **A man is not saved, nor is he lost, against his will. Whoever is at the helm of your ship is there with your consent.**

How could this happen?

I knew, in my heart, Jesus revealed Satan as the Author of Lies. But in my soul, when I saw the Banner of Benevolence flying over his ship, I believed his promises. Why are we so quick to trust the infamous Deceiver, but it takes us so much longer to put our faith in Him Whose name is *Truth*? In deciding the steps we take, words we speak, even directions we pursue at any given moment of our lives, we often follow the lead of our soul and not our spirit, our head and not our heart. I believe knowing the difference is of crucial importance.

Most people, even scientists, psychologists, atheists, and New Agers, agree that humans are more than just a body with bones and blood. We acknowledge our mind is much more than just a brain with synapses and signals. We know there's *more* to ourselves, but many, admittedly, don't know what the *more* is.

Your divine design sets you supremely apart from all other creations of God. Made in His image and likeness, you are a three-part being with the capabilities to know Him, hear His voice, and follow His beautiful manifest for your life.

The Bible is chock-full of astounding discoveries and describes your unique design and qualities in an extraordinary fashion. In a few words, you are a spirit (*pneuma*), you have a soul (*psuche*), and you live in a body (*soma*). If we put them into rank, your body, or flesh, with all its appetites and constant needs, is the lowest part of you. Identified as your "base nature," your flesh demands pleasure and ease above all else. But any contentment is abysmally temporary. Your flesh is never satisfied.

Next up is your soul: your mind, free will, and emotions. This part of you is like the switcher on a train track. As ideas, paradigms, opportunities, and so forth are coming to you, your soul determines upon which tracks they and, accordingly, you will travel. Will you take the high road or the low road? What or whom will you chase after? As new words and theories reach the train yard, which will you adopt as your own, and which will you send on their way?

As an athlete trains his mind to yield to disciplines for his benefit, you must train your head to submit to your heart. If not, your unrenewed soul can think much higher of itself than it should and may completely derail God's plan for your life.

The highest part of you is your spirit. This is the part of your design, which is most like God's image and likeness. Your spirit, your heart, is the true you and alone holds the capacity to know your Creator. Just as your ears cannot see light and your eyes cannot hear a sound, neither can your mind know God; only your spirit can do that.

Your soul and body are meant to serve your spirit as you sail with God, fulfill your manifest, and reach your homeport. Here's a simple way to understand our divine design.

You're Looking for Me

Imagine you're making your way to my home for a visit. As you arrive, you don't speak to my house, nor do you expect my house to talk to you. You've not come to spend time with or communicate with the building in which I live. No, once you've located where I live, our visit begins when you engage with me, the one who lives on the inside.

Your body is only your house. The real you, the part of you which is eternal, created in the image and the likeness of God, though invisible, lives on the inside.

Your spirit, the true you, is the one your friends are searching for when they stop by. You can easily see how we may keep some people standing on the porch while others we welcome into our hearts.

Fatefully, some will invest thousands, if not millions of dollars, and a lifetime of effort, educating their souls and fine-tuning their bodies, but never learn to train, build, and maximize the most important part of their being: their spirit. Much like spending all of your time, energy, and resources repairing and renovating your house while ignoring the health and development of the resident who suffers inside.

Jesus went so far as to say, "Listen! I am standing at the door, knocking; if you hear My voice and open the door, I will come into you and eat with you, and you with Me."

I'm probably not the only one, but I'm still embarrassed to tell you. Sometimes, when I know a solicitor is at my door, I hide. Not in the closet or anything extreme, but I make sure they can't see I'm home. It's rude of me and selfish, I know, but I don't want to deal with hearing the spiel and having to tell them no.

Sadly, this is the image a lot of folks have of Jesus: He's a religion peddler, a solicitor of salvation, or, some old tired, rambling, faded friend of the family they'd just as soon forget about than invite inside for fellowship.

Let me assure you, friend, Jesus isn't knocking on your door to sell you something or to take something from you. He's on your porch with the most Life-giving gift you'll ever be offered. More than anything, He wants to flood your heart with all He alone can give: forgiveness, life, healing, peace, joy, and freedom from pirates!

Not a few will hide from God and leave the One Who made them standing on the porch for no other reason than having never learned how to open the door of their hearts. Others, like Adam, with eyes wide open, boldly post their notice, *God is not welcome here!*

The Usurper has profitably convinced an awful lot of people that walking in the spirit, in friendship with their Maker, is a figment of their imagination. Respectfully, my imagination could have never come up with the immeasurable goodness and gracious love God has shown me. He's beyond all we can ask or ever dream possible!

Easy Prey

When anchoring his strongholds in our souls, the Sinister Squatter leverages our spiritual blindness to his advantage. One reason the human journey can be so difficult, deceptive, and, frankly, disappointing is because we often settle to live, or, more accurately, survive, from our lower nature, our appetites and soulful cravings. When all the while, we're invited to thrive from our highest nature: God's Life dwelling in our newborn spirit—imparted to us when we welcome His Son, Jesus Christ, onto our ship.

The smirking Oppressor delights in watching God's greatest creation, Humankind, merely surviving on bugs and dry kernels, pecking around like overfed chickens. Unlike masses of humanity, Satan, the Prince of Pirates, grasps the mystery of our design.

We're created to soar like golden eagles in the high places of God's glory, Light and Life. Here's how we become earthbound.

An Unfriendly Handshake

"Hey! How you doin', buddy?! How you doin'?!" Doug hollered, shooting his turgid hand into my face so as to not be denied.

"Hey, Doug," I replied to my fellow mucho-macho college classmate. I trustingly put my hand into his for what I thought was going to be a friendly handshake. I believed we were on agreed terms of kindness. I fell for it. Literally.

As he took my hand, all at once, he sneered, tightened his grip, and jerked me toward him, causing me to stumble forward. I ended up with my head planted on his chest, while he's still strangling my hand and laughing down at me.

This is the bullish way of the Pirate. What began as a trivial idea or thought has now become a life-leading stronghold. Inch by inch, he lulls and pulls you into a place where you're no longer at the helm of your ship. The Thug contrives your willingness to put your hand into his. Once you accept his invitation, he laughingly yanks you into a position of inescapable submission.

Here's a drop-anchor truth you must understand: *The enemy doesn't* **find** *strongholds, he* **builds** *them up from granted footholds.*

The *foothold* the pirate gained when you yielded to his temptation or idea, when you trustingly put your hand into his, has now been fortified into a *stronghold*, a new way of thinking, a new habit, a new normal.

I'm sure you've heard it said, "Sin will take you further than you wanted to go, leave you longer than you wanted to stay, and cost you more than you wanted to pay." As it was with our forefather, Adam, the Intruder wants far more from you than just your present cooperation. If given a *foothold*, his next step is to strengthen his grip into a *stronghold*. Where he's headed with all of this is to, at last, lower your flag and hoist his colors over your life, declaring to all, "This one is mine!"

Setting the Trap

If we had a few minutes at the end of science class, and if Mr. Folsom was in good humor, we enjoyed running the old Graflex movie projector in reverse, watching the images on the screen run, swim, or bloom backward.

If we take its three frames in reverse, we can do the same in watching the developmental progression of a foothold growing into a stronghold.

In Frame One, like a seed blown by the wind, a thought, an idea, or a word finds its way into the soil of your soul. This happens to each of us hundreds of times each day. Many inklings and ideas are harmless and require no real deliberation whatsoever.

Some seeds of thoughts, however, carry a significant measure of impact. These considerations capture your attention and carry with them the power to influence your words, your actions, and your entire life if you permit it.

If they're good seeds then, by all means, continue to cultivate them and watch all God can do in and through your life. But if they're harmful or selfish, we're exhorted, in God's Word, to bring them into captivity and submit each one to the obedience of God's Word and Spirit. Like a flower-choking weed, root the destructive thoughts out. When we allow any seeds to gather roots, we progress to frame two.

The concept of mind mapping can help us see how a stronghold grows in Frame Two. It works like this:

In the middle of your paper, write a word or idea you'd like to develop. Then, rippling outward from your chosen word, draw lines, like the spokes on a wheel shooting out from its hub. On the end points of each spoke, write associations, other ideas, or whatever your mind can imagine germinating from your seed-thought or word.

You're using your mind to add images and supportive arguments to your original thought. In doing so, you're personalizing it by imagining yourself speaking the word or acting on whatever the seed may suggest. No longer is it an isolated idea or random thought that can easily be cast down or let to pass on by down the track. You have agreed to let the seed take root in the soil of your soul. Like a stronghold, it will now draw nourishment from your attention and imagination.

Rehearse these images long enough and you arrive at the fatal Frame Three. The fledgling stronghold will work its way out of your imagination and right into your attitudes, words, and actions. It's much easier to remove a sprig of oak before it grows and strengthens into an established tree.

My rage-filled reaction to getting knocked down on the basketball court is Exhibit A of the force of a ripening stronghold. I had willingly welcomed the pirate to board my vessel. I then cooperated, seed by seed, as he methodically poisoned my ship with shame and embarrassment, anger and resentment, bitterness and disappointment. I cultivated these destructive thoughts until they became flowering attitudes and paradigms. In the perfectly timed and tempered situation, the stronghold ignited and exploded like a stick of dynamite!

Long before I understood the process of thoughts becoming imaginations, and imaginations growing into life-shaping strongholds, I allowed a horrible idea to take root in my soul.

Set-Up

I was a shy and compliant kid and avoided conflict at all costs. I felt high on the beam if I learned I had pleased my teachers or parents. So, when I looked straight into my mother's eyes and screamed, "Why don't you just shut up!" it was, to describe it mildly, concussive.

I was thirteen. During one of the usual reminders my mom would give me to finish my daily chores, the pirate, ever so subtly, began sprinkling his seeds. He scattered out a few toxic ideas to my agitated and vulnerable soul.

> *Why do I always have to do everything around here?*
> *Who does she think she is always bossing me around like I'm a prisoner?*
> *I'm not gonna take it anymore!*

My mother was no nag. I genuinely needed reminding. My dad often pointed out, "Arthur, you'd forget your behind if it weren't glued on!"

For days, like the boiling frog, I stewed in these ideas, images, and feelings. Soon, though always and only in my mind, they became my normal and consistent response to my precious mother's directives. Then, the sly sower lodged a critical seed in my soul. He secured his foothold with this doozy of an idea: *Why don't you just tell her to shut up?!*

I shuttered. I would never talk back to my mother. She was kind, always considerate and respectful toward me. Besides all of this, there was my dad, who was head-over-heels in love with her. Long before I came along, he'd pledged himself to protect her life and dignity. He'd never stand for any sass toward his wife, especially from one of her own children.

Though I flinched at the idea, I didn't regard it enough to root it out. I should have simply forgotten all about it, but I didn't. Slowly but surely, each time my mom said anything to me about my chores, I'd water the seeds by squaring my shoulders and, with fierce intention, telling her off. Oh, make no mistake about it, my plan was to no more than innocently imagine it.

I'm not hurting anybody just thinking about it.

Like all experienced farmers, the pirate is patient. With his seeds and my cooperation, hurtful strongholds were rooted in my soul. He knew it was only a matter of time before they bore fruit.

Over the next couple of weeks, one fiery ember at a time, I allowed my mother's directives to fuel my hungry rage. No matter how kind or patient she'd speak, my mind would flurry with inward dialogue, rebuttals; shameful comments, and selfish mind trips.

I was sure I'd never actually do it. But that was because I didn't understand how strongholds grow from footholds in our souls. The potential and power of the seed were waiting for the right moment, the right conditions, to break through into words and actions.

Shut Up!

The afternoon was so hot the road ahead looked like a wavy mirage. After a long plod from school, I made it home, exhausted and edgy. Like a usurping wild bramble, choking out the life of a beautiful flower, my rotten attitude toward my mom had grown from a facile foothold to a significant stronghold. The trap was set. My poisoned temper was waiting for a trigger.

Have you ever been in a situation, maybe a conversation, when, all at once, you're aware you had seen it coming? You had rehearsed it and now it was happening? It becomes irresistible to follow through with the script.

I was the kind of hungry that makes you feel hollow on the inside. Agitated and bone tired, I was, in a word, assailable.

Sweat soaking every thread of my *Star Wars* T-shirt, it felt good to slam the screen door behind me as I dawdled into the house.

"Hello, Arthur," my mom greeted me with her familiar kindness and care. "How was your day?"

"Fine," I grunted faintly, stomping my way to the kitchen without so much as a glance toward the woman who'd risk her life for mine and who had worked awfully hard, every single day, to ensure it was a good one.

"Are you doing good?" she lifted her voice to extend her gracious care to my welfare.

Klump!

"Hungry." I cadenced my ill-tempered sighs with the hard landing of my pile of books on the kitchen table. I gave no concern to the salt shaker that had fallen over when my books struck the table.

Oh, well.

On my way to the long-sought fridge, I heard, from a distant room, my mom's predicted instructions.

"Please be sure and use Comet when you clean the sinks today." She halfway sang, her chirpy tone thumping the thorn in my already tender temper. "We have guests coming to visit us this evening."

Just like that. The ground cracked open and the fatal fruit broke through.

I opened the refrigerator and just stared into it in blood-boiling silence. All at once, we're in the middle of the scenario the pirate and I had scripted. By now, like a GIF on a perpetual loop, I'd played this rebel rising over and over in my mind so many times, I couldn't escape its inevitable end. It had me in a stronghold!

"Did you hear me, honey?" she asked, walking into the kitchen. My having heard her was genuinely open to question due to my non-response.

And . . . action!

SPLACK!

Without deliberation between my head and my heart, the clapperboard clapped! As in my countless rehearsals, I squared my shoulders, glared at her straight in the eyes, and yelled, "Please, Mom, why don't you just shut up?!"

Like a pirate's cutlass had pierced her heart, the sweetest woman in my life, slack-jawed, stepped back from me with bewilderment in her eyes, revealing pure pain. Instantly, I wished I could take those terrible words back into my mouth. Too late.

Like a determined root, erupting through a concrete sidewalk, my flesh wouldn't be satisfied until I heard, out loud and in action, the words I had embedded in my soul. She'd heard them, too, loud and clear. And there was someone else.

In my sapped and sordid arrival, I hadn't noticed my dad was home. There he stood, in the doorway, steel-faced and staring at me, much like the Hulk one second after he had turned green. He'd seen and heard the entire outburst. Not good. Not good at all.

With his jutted jaw and his tongue driven into the top of his mouth, he leaped at me like some ferocious lion covering his prize. The next thing I knew, I was lifted up between heaven and earth by the temper of a man whose love for his wife was more than I could have possibly comprehended.

"You may talk to me that way," the enraged husband growled through clenched teeth and fists. "You may talk to your dog that way. You may even get away with talking to other people that way. But let me make one thing flawlessly clear so that you'll never be confused about this again." He jolted me higher as he adjusted his grip on the part of my collar he was using for his handle.

"You cannot and will not, not now, not ever, speak to my wife that way!" He finally breathed. "She was here long before you were, and she'll be here long after you're gone!"

Heaving, we shot blazing bullets into each other's eyes for a long time; his full of fire, mine full of fear.

I was, indeed, afraid of my father's fury, but I was more horrified of the soul-shaping power the pirate had gained in my life.

As it was with my brain-rupturing blow-up on the basketball court, when I screamed at my mother, I felt I was watching someone else's life.

Increasingly contemptuous, my heart was being pushed down and buried beneath my new destructive attitudes and behaviors.

I'd go on to adopt any number of the practices and ways of the pirates to whom I'd yielded the helm of my ship. Granted footholds can quickly become powerful strongholds.

After he apologized for what he called an overreaction, my dad grounded me for a couple of weeks. He took away from me what seemed at the time every privilege he could think of. I was required but also desired to apologize to my mom for my outburst of anger.

All of this was the least of my concerns. I ached, deep in my heart, knowing this stronghold in my life had hurt my mother. I'd love to say I learned my lesson and pulled down the destructive temper right away.

Sadly, this pirate would stay on board for years to come and would often hurt people I cared about. For a long stint of my journey, I sailed under the flag of the pirate who bore the moniker *Rage*.

REFITTED

As hunted criminals, pirates couldn't swagger down to their local shipyard and put in an order for a new ship. The vessels they captured that they determined would serve them well were refitted, repurposed, and renamed according to the new captain's preferences, practices, and plans.

I was sick with fear, standing at the place and the moment I'd been dreading for the last eight hours: in front of my dealer's house.

I can count on one hand the times I've trembled involuntarily; this was one of them. As I pulled open the rusty, torn, mostly unhinged screen door, it moaned for being bothered. Before I could knock, I heard the faint but familiar mishmash of sounds.

I'd been on the other side of this door enough times to recognize the shuffling of boxes, furniture, and feet. Andy was hastily straightening up for things to appear neat and normal.

Long, deep breath.

I tapped lightly on the hollow and bruised interior door. It had replaced the heavy exterior door long before my first knock almost three years earlier. I huddled pensively among the many cracked and chipped tombs of plants dead by neglect.

The flickers of the working half of an eroded string of tiny blue Christmas lights, held by push pins, shrouded the door, further aggravating my nausea. I hoped my truckling would dampen the anticipated keel hauling.

With a cocaine-driven excess of confidence and in a rushing cloud of cannabis, the pocket-sized pusher threw open the door. To look at Andy was to forget to breathe. He was old, stiff, cranky, and drug-worn, inside and out. His only brother described the drugster's face as having caught on fire, and somebody put it out with an icepick. He was tiny and wiry with a sunken chest contributing to his distinctive and disruptive cough.

"Hey," fell out of my mouth with a long and groveling exhale.

"Art, it's you." He breathed deeply to relax, spurring a long chain of smoker's hack. "Man, you look horrible," he assessed, wiping his mouth with his sleeve. "Come on in. Let's get high! Doobie? Or snow show?"

I shook my head, avoiding his permanently angry eyes.

"I have some really bad news to tell you," I said, gulping for breath and fighting to hold back tears …

I went on to tell Andy some of the worst news I could give, for him and for me. Before I recount for you what I told him, let me bring you up to speed on how I arrived at one of the most terrifying scenes of my life.

All Hands on Deck

On a Monday morning in early February 1981, a rare and heavy fog wrapped itself around our tired and dirty city of Riverside, California. After a stressful weekend, I hadn't slept very well. A bolt of adrenaline nailed me the instant I opened my eyes. The epiphanic reminder of what I was about to do struck my conscience, shocking me thoroughly awake.

Like most other days, I woke to the same pirate presence I went to sleep with: worry and dread. I was free from their endless nagging only while I slept.

I sat on the side of my bed, hoping the change of posture would relieve the dull throbbing in my clenched jaws from grinding my teeth through the night. Wringing my hands, I replayed the plan, for the thousandth time, of how my morning was to go.

Don't do this.

Even from its imprisoned isolation, my heart was still trying to save me.

This is the only day you've got. The pirate pressed. *Don't freak out.*

I'd carefully studied the predictable schedules of our school's quad monitors, security guards, and teachers. Mondays were favorable due to the absence of most, if not all, adults whom I needed to avoid at the back entrance of the shop quad.

Fretting over every parlous detail, I mapped out my entry route, confirmed the faces and the places of each exchange, riffled through my top-grade explanations for the slim odds I may be caught or questioned. And, as usual, I pledged, *This is absolutely the last time you're doin' this, man—ever!*

As I had done many times over the previous two years, I confirmed my parents had left for work and that my sister and brother were otherwise engaged. Evading my mirror to steer clear of the irritation of looking eye-to-eye with myself, I restively secured my load.

I recall when the idea snapped into my mind to protect the product from the soggy weather by double wrapping each baggie. I grimaced at the thought of facing my dealer if his goods were ruined because of poor packaging.

Satisfied I had done what I could, I stuffed all of my tools and paraphernalia back into their hiding spot at the top of my closet. I'm wincing as I tell you that I began then to carefully fill up my pockets with marijuana, cocaine, speed, and hash.

My hands, my life, my talents, and time had been used, just a few years earlier, to help people. I cleaned yards for elderly folks in our church and washed dogs and cars for families in my neighborhood. I had sung in my dad's youth choir and was involved in ministry with my mom. I'd enjoyed doing my chores at home and was always happy whenever my dad would invite me to help him with his work. Now, doing good deeds, serving others and the like, never even entered my mind.

My life had been refitted, repurposed, and renamed by the pirate, who had taken over my ship. He'd promised to help me succeed in life and to give me friends. Now, for my part of the bargain, I lived for myself and for the pirate, of course, to whom I had pledged my loyalty. No longer was I called Arthur the Helpful but Arthur the Harmful.

I was sailing the seas under a new commander and under a new flag. My gifts and passions—my crew—were no longer in favor of God and others; instead, I was using and being used to ruin lives.

Do you remember "painter's pants?" They were a fashion thing when I was in high school. All of their extra pockets made them handy when I needed to covertly carry a large quantity of drugs.

After a few years of carrying and delivering, I had gained Andy's. So, on this particular haul, I stuffed nearly a thousand dollars worth of merchandise into my pockets.

Ordinarily, when I left my house, I'd just let the front door slam behind me. On this worrisome morning, books in hand, I slowly and thoughtfully closed the door, listening for the click. It would separate me from the sanctity and safety of my home, my family. As I carefully paced my walk to school, my head quarreled with my heart every step of the way.

The comforting blanket of fog had thinned by the time I reached the back gate of my school. Dark, heavy clouds loomed low, moving freely, immune to rules and boundaries.

The back gate was my preferred way in, not only because it typically had the least amount of teachers and admins, but it was also the nearest access from my house.

I slowed for a few strides as my calculated route brought me across the center and left field of the baseball diamond. I glanced over my shoulder to see my trail, where I had broken the seal of the overnight dusting of dew. I reached the gate.

Oh no! What's going on?

On this day, I wasn't the only one who preferred the back door.

"Ev-AANS!" the security guard sing-songed my last name like an impatient friend who had been waiting on me but wanted me to know he wasn't—my friend, that is. He had indeed been waiting.

I was startled to hear my name called by someone I had seen before but didn't know. A thousand hounds were immediately at my heels on this cold and misty morning. My ears were set on fire as I blushed to bright red and endured the flush of those pins and needles right before the breaking of a sweat.

"Yes, sir," I gushed with forced and syrupy kindness. "Good morning!"

At the moment, it all seems legit, but the person without fear and with nothing to hide can peer right through the sham. My head was whirling. My stomach was lurching.

How does he know my name?

"No jacket? Aren't you cold out here?" Smileless and flat, he sought my well-being. "You've probably got an extra shirt or cap in your pockets, huh?"

"Yeah, I'll be fine." Breaking eye contact as quickly as possible, I held my coerced smile. "Thanks."

I lowered my load of books closer to my pockets and kept pressing toward the quad and my first-period class. I was working on getting out of earshot, beyond the reach of his voice.

"Well, Evans," he called gently and calmly, "let's have a quick chat this morning."

He pointed directly at me and then slowly, with the same long finger, redirected me to the outlying bathrooms at the near side of the baseball field.

"Won't take long." From underneath the bill of his badge cap, his unblinking eyes pierced mine.

Done. Cooked. Busted. A hemmed-in hoodlum.

I tried to throw him off by appearing to be agitated: *For no reason, whatsoever, I'm being directed by a school security guard to come and "have a quick chat," which will likely make me late for class.*

"Whatever," I replied.

My life was passing before my eyes. My chest and throat were caving in. I was living my worst fear, gravely aware any chance I had of escaping this quagmire was gone.

What now?

My worries far outweighed my cargo.

He let me go into the cold cinder block, dimly lit, no-doors-on-the-stalls, use-at-your-own-risk bathroom alone.

Uninterrupted, he continued to casually greet students heading to class. It was clear he was allowing me time to ponder what was going on and showing me he was calm and comfortable in this situation. In a blink, I could see my entire life derailed. I could envision myself set off to the disqualified side as the world rolled on.

He was a good man, as you'll see. I think he was attempting to lessen my visible agony and lower my guard.

"I know your mom and dad," he informed me as he finally stepped into the foul-smelling men's room.

"Oh, yeah?" I blubbered, moiling and miserable.

"Yeah, they helped my brother out not too long ago." He dipped his head as a nod of honor. "They're pastors, right?"

"Yeah. Well, kinda." My brain felt scrambled. "They're m-ministers. I guess you could say they're p-pastors. Yeah. They … help people, for sure."

"Yeah, they're real nice." He shifted his face and feet at the same time. "I've been watching you for the last few weeks, Art," he revealed. "That's your name? Art?"

I nodded, desperately trying to find my filed but fled explanations.

You prepared for this, you idiot! the pirate chimed.

"I know somebody's gotchoo," he appealed with undeniable sincerity of concern.

"What do you mean?" I scoffed with a flick of my chin.

"You belong to somebody. You're a peddler? A carrier. Right?" He raised his voice and smiled, big, as though someone had given him the answers to all the questions. "The bag man! You the holler for the dollar!"

"I don't understand what you mean," I admitted with genuine ignorance of the terms.

"Listen, you can dump all the games with me. I know you've got a load today and you're not leaving this bathroom 'til every pocket is empty."

Oh my God. Oh my God. My mind was frenzied, frozen.

I smirked and jutted my chin as high as I could and slammed my books down onto one of the rusted sinks.

A heavy, thick, long sigh of exasperation. I glared.

"I wanna help you, man, not hurt you. I'm one of the good guys."

I was in a straitjacket of fear and anger, fastened with a padlock of shame. No. Way. Out. I stared at the ground for the longest time, waiting for a meteor to smash into the building or an earthquake to pull the floor, and me with it, into oblivion.

"What are you gonna do?" I slumped, lacking both the will or the power to look up.

"What am I gonna do?" he rebuffed, tapping his chest with raised fingers. "I'll tell you what I'm gonna do. I'm gonna protect this school from people like you!" He maintained his cold stare for punctuation. Satisfied he'd stung my soul, he mellowed just a touch. "The better question is, what are you going to do?"

With his security guard mandate, but with mercy in his eyes, he ordered, "Empty every pocket right here."

He pointed to and then tapped with his gloved index finger on the cracked and corroded concrete ledge running across the top of the row of toilets.

Head down with eyes hidden, I pulled out baggie after baggie and balls of foil from my pockets. The growing pile of drugs inflicted grief upon the security guard. His face changed from stern to sad.

The sting of failure and the angst of the unknown pained me with every delivery I made to the ledge.

"You got any idea how foolish you are?" he drilled.

I wasn't halfway finished unpacking.

"We're waaay past Possession, here," he informed me with an intense wag of his head. "There's no way I could say, all you had is Possession. This is way too much for just you. You understand what I'm sayin'?"

"No. No, sir. I don't," I replied, unnerved as I continued my inglorious task, sicker, and shorter of breath by the second. "What do you mean?"

"What we have here, muh man, is Possession with the Intent to Distribute," he pronounced. "Art, this is very serious! This is felony activity, here! You could go to jail for a very long time, and it's likely your folks will have to pay fines. Big time!"

If he was aiming to frighten me, it was working, a hundred times over!

He didn't seem the least bit satisfied revealing he was up to speed with federal laws. I saw genuine pain grimace his face as he realized what he had on his hands. In his own way, he was in as much turmoil as I was. If I ever imagined what it might feel like to walk the plank, this would be it.

The considerable sum of substances, stacked on the ledge, looked strange to me, unfamiliar even, in the unwelcome light of a sensible person's judgment.

How did I ever think that I could pull this off? I condemned myself. *You're so stupid! You're dead.*

My world crumbled under the weight of worry, embarrassment, and the fear of punishment. I crumpled into a blubbering mess on the bathroom floor and scooted against the wall, curling every finger and toe as tightly as I could, trying to disappear.

My imagination had me dressed in prison blues and locked behind bars. Once again, I could see my parents' flabbergasted faces talking to me on an old, dirty phone through a thick pane of glass.

"Well." He filled his chest with air and let it drop suddenly with an audible exhale. "from where I'm standing, it looks to me like you've got two options."

Buried in torment, I could barely hear him.

"You and I, and all of this," he proposed, waving his hand over the mound of drugs to reemphasize the magnitude of my foolishness, "can get in my car and go straight to the police station. Or ..."

"Sir! Please! Please don't make me do that!" I pleaded through tears. "It would kill my mother! I'm so sorry for doing this. I don't want to go to jail! There's gotta be another way! Please! Please."

"Or." He held up both of his hands toward me as if trying to hold me together. "Or you have another choice."

He raised his chin and eyebrows, assessing me from the bottom of his eyes, conveying there would be a cost with the next possibility, too.

I rearranged myself on the floor. I found relief in filling my hands with hair on both sides of my head and gradually pulling harder and harder.

"Okay." I braced and strained to hear every word.

"You can get up from there, and with your own hands, dump every bit of this crap into the toilet and flush it."

It would take a few seconds for the gravity of his offer to punch through to my befuddled brain. When reality jumped the gap, the magnitude of the trouble I was facing knocked the air out of me again.

Andy.

Groaning, I sank back down to the lowest place I could find on the disgusting floor.

"I can't do that. It's not mine." I felt empty and hopeless, as I could see the sharks circling below. No help in sight. "He'll kill me! I can't!"

"You got no other options, muh man," he said, failing to wrangle the power of my imagination. "He's not gonna kill you. That's not gonna happen."

"You don't know him," I begged. "He'll do it!"

"Well." He nodded toward the knoll of narcotics. "This is mine now."

He picked up a handful of baggies and shook them at me as though I was seeing them for the first time.

"Are you thinking I'm just gonna let you stuff all this back into your pockets, and promise me that you'll be good from now on? You know that's not gonna happen!"

Exasperated, he hurled the dope back to the pile on the ledge.

"So, you and me, we can take it to the police, or you can get up from there and take it to the toilet." He crossed his big badge-bearing arms. "You choose."

Worse than any whoopin' I'd ever gotten was the nonstop head wagging, mutterings of dismay, and the cutting side-eye glances of disbelief and disapproval from the school policeman as I tanked Andy's merchandise, baggie by baggie, dollar by dollar.

After the final flush, waving fistfuls of plastic baggies and balls of foil, he predicted, "I'll bet you'll never forget this day! Huh?"

He didn't put the empty containers into the trash, they went into his jacket pocket, ratcheting up my anxiety.

"Are you gonna tell my parents?" I was anguished. "My coaches?"

"That's for me to know and for you to worry about!"

He raised his chin and his brows, motioning with his hands like he was tossing something up and into the wind. "Maybe I will. Maybe I won't."

"You'd better not let me hear of you skipping even one class, today." He locked his eyes on mine. "Now, get goin'."

Trembling in worry, I dragged myself out of the jury-less courtroom. He had effectively exposed and inflamed my most sensitive nerves. Nothing else mattered; nothing else even made it onto the screen of my mind for the rest of my school day. Like your tongue perpetually probing your sore or broken tooth, my thoughts were fixated on images soon to be my reality.

Pirate's Breath

"Art, it's you. Man, you look horrible! Come on in. Let's get high."

I shook my head.

"I got some really bad news to tell you." I could barely get the words out. My mouth felt stuffed with cotton.

He pinched his lips together and with a flinch of his head and raised, ignited eyes, he shot me a warning across the bow.

"All right." Andy turned and punched the On button of his stereo, filling the room with Santana's "Let It Shine," adding to my agitation.

"Sit right there." He pointed to the army-cot green, fake-velvet beanbag chair. I hated sitting in it; it was terribly hard to climb out of.

On his way down, falling tiredly onto the worn and faded suede couch, he nabbed what he called his "sugar box." It was a matchbox-sized silver slide box always loaded with three or four grams of cocaine. He kept it with him at all times as his five-hundred-dollar-a-day master mandated.

In a timeless torpor, he was already a good way down the white-line highway. All the same, he jerkily slid open the shiny lid, loaded his coke nail, and paid his pirate. This was followed by a fit of sniffing and rubbing his eyes and face like he was scouring, which I thought would never end.

"Whus goin' on?" he asked, regaining enough cognition to find me in his blur.

He kicked his feet up onto the coffee table, scattering all kinds of containers, utensils, and sundries, leaving me to have to look across the dirty bottoms of his boots to see his face. This little swipe, along with crossing his arms and tapping his fingers impatiently on his elbow, were some of his orgulous tactics of power and superiority.

71

"I got busted, today, at school," I confessed, with pleading eyes. "I had to flush everything down the toilet."

Just like that, he joined me in my world of pandemonium.

The forty-five-year-old spindly pusher could only glare at me through his bleak and torpid eyes. His mind was grappling to catch a grip on any one of the scads of thoughts zooming in on him from every direction.

Like a boiling kettle finally blows its whistle, he erupted off of the couch and screamed at me at the top of his lungs. He was a small, frail, worn-out man, so the top of his lungs was like the roar of a mouse.

He pelted me with question after question, without giving me any chance to answer.

"All of it? Who busted you? A teacher? A cop?" He was waving his hands and closing in on me with every demand. "Are you lyin' to me? How much are we talkin' 'bout here? What happened? Who else knows about this? How much did you lose? Just pot. Right? No nodge. Right? Where were you? Are you @#$%& kiddin' me?"

Heaving and hacking, his fetid breath and slavering down on my face, he stood over me shaking, seething. His nose almost touching mine, he bared his clenched, smog-yellow teeth in some animalistic display of power.

"A-a-all of it. Ev-everything. All you gave me on … on … Saturday!" I explained, raising my hands and my voice only slightly. "The security guard at school was waiting for me at the back gate of …"

"What kinda idiot are you?" he condemned. "Who would take that much to school all at one time?

Stupefied, all I could do was stare in gutless wonder, hoping to wake up from a bad dream.

"This can't be happenin'! This ain't real!" He raised up and began to pace like a savage hyena. "You're lyin' to me, man! You muggin' me right now!"

Oh no.

The idea of Andy thinking I was stealing from him had not entered my mind. I had come ready to suffer the fallout of losing the drugs, the dollars, but not to defend my dealings.

"No!" I tried to get up. "No, I'm not muggin' you! I flushed everything down the toilet!"

That was it! The quarter dropped into the whack-a-mole machine.

His eyes narrowed, and his neck arched as he filled his lungs.

"Aaargh!" He looked like he couldn't decide if he wanted to grab my hair, punch my face, or kick me. So, red-faced and screaming, he did quite a bit of all of it.

And I'm stuck in the stinky, coffee-stained, inescapable beanbag chair!

"You @#$%&! After everything I've done for you?! Nobody steals from me!" He kicked my right shin with the point of his boot, stealing what little breath I had left. "Nobody!"

All I could do was shudder and try to protect myself.

"I gotta eat, too, Jack! You're not smart enough to get my money, you @#$%&! Who you with? You tryin' to cut me out! Where's my dope? Where's ... my ... money?!"

In pulse with every word, he clubbed the side of my head with the biting knuckles of his small fist. He caught me by my hair as I had never been grabbed before. I thought he would pull it out of my head. So, I followed the pain and stood up. Bad move. The five-foot-eight-inch, hundred-and-ten pound bully construed this as a threat.

"Oh, you think so, huh?" He growled, his jaundiced eyes, wild and scurrying. "You gonna do me now? You @#$%&!! First, you mug me now you gonna beat me down?"

I had just turned seventeen years old. Andy was close to fifty. I was taller, heavier, and stronger, but I had no intention of fighting back. I just wanted this to be over. It was far from it.

"You can go to hell, Art, and tell 'em who sent ya!" Without moving his feet, he careened backward, toward the couch, toppling an expensive glass bong.

Crash!

It shattered on the table and scattered to the floor! Lurching in an effort to catch his treasured pipe, he fell, palms down, onto shards of glass.

"Argh! Now look whatcha done!" More scurrilous cawing.

On his knees, hunched over and not diverting his eyes from the glass-pierced palm of his left hand, he wedged his right hand underneath the single cushion of the couch and brought out a gun. I'd never seen it before. So slowly, as if he was evaluating every frame of his life, he turned his frozen eyes and trembling gun, stoically, to my face.

Mental, emotional, physical—every gear slipped into neutral. Frictionless. The late-afternoon sunlight colandered through the filthy windows and tattered drapes, spotlighting dust and cat dander floating by. The smallish faded black-and-white of John and Yoko, in its valentine-red plastic frame, hung lonely, crooked, and preposterously too high.

The solacing fog that had accompanied my walk to school earlier in the morning randomly flickered across my mind. The stale, sour reek of marijuana and hash smoke infused in every surface of this trap house would embed itself into my soul for years to come.

I became aware my heart was pounding. I heard its punch as much as I felt it heaving my chest, fighting to keep up. I could make out Gary Wright, the old Spooky Tooth member, singing "Dream Weaver." This was the first and only time I've had a gun pointed at my head.

It looked similar to a model pistol I'd had as a kid. I could see its handle made of beautiful wood and the steely color of the metal; it was no toy. A few years down the road, struggling to outrun this memory, I thought it would be helpful to know precisely with what Andy had threatened my life. It turns out it was a single-action .45 Long Colt.

He was in a state of wrath where the only words he could find were shameful. I'll spare you any further expression of his vile language; it permeated his heart and his house. After his blue streak, his reason returned slightly.

His shaking gun and warped red face two inches from mine, low and slow, he said through gritted teeth, "You screwed up, t'day, boy. I'm gonna blow your head off."

I didn't grasp it then, and I don't mean Andy, but I'd come face to face with the pirate whose heavy boot was on my neck.

"No!" No!" Pain seized my stomach. I dropped to my knees and doubled over. Feeling the point of Andy's gun rapping on the back of my head, I shuddered and forcibly twisted away. I buried my face and hands into the beanbag chair.

Oh, God! My God! My God!

The heat was suffocating. Like breathing through a stir straw in a steam room. Overwhelmed, gasping and dizzy, I blacked out.

Disoriented, I was startled by a string of shouts from another room in the small house. I thought I was in my bedroom, and the loud voice I heard was my mother's, calling me to get up for school.

My face, arms, and hands became super itchy. I think it was because a gallon of my blood was rushing around trying to figure out where in my body it was most needed the most. What I imagined was an army of black ants was swarming me.

As I reconnected to reality, I was lying face down in the greasy, grassy-like shag carpet. I've thanked God many times since that moment that I was not alone with this man.

"Andy! Andy?!" The noise and commotion had reached Andy's girlfriend, Sheila. "What in God's name are you doin'?!"

She bolted into the den, yelling, "Don't point that gun at him! Andy! Put it down! Andy! Andy!"

He didn't flinch.

"He's cuttin' us out, baby! Nobody's gonna cut us out!" He put the point of his gun less than an inch from my eyes. "Where's my money?!" he demanded slowly.

"I swear! I flushed it! I wouldn't cut you out, Andy. The security guard was waiting for me and took me into the bathroom. He told me that if I didn't put all of it …"

He pushed the gun downward, making it press into my cheek just below my eye.

Sickened, I cowered on the floor.

"I don't believe you! You're lying to me!"

You read in the papers or your daily Yahoo feed about things like this happening all the time. I knew an angry drug dealer with a gun could, and would, kill. I closed my eyes and consigned my head into my shaking hands and imagined the faces of my family as they heard the news of what had happened to their son and brother.

I wonder what Ken is doing right now. If only Mom and Dad knew where I was and what was happening to me.

While others were going about their ordinary Monday afternoon, I was about to die.

Rapt in Rage

Sheila was kind to the other two peddlers who worked for Andy, and to me. She was tender-hearted and frail but could be tough when she needed to be. She was forever putting on fresh lipstick, of which most usually ended up on her teeth, and never happy with the outcome of her latest tussle with her dirty, stringy blond hair. She seemed to be in a constant state of repair.

She had navigated a long and intense journey of abuse throughout her growing-up years and would often suffer ill treatment from Andy. Sheila is the reason I came to warmly appreciate the character of Nancy in Charles Dickens's *Oliver Twist.*

While listening to her accounts of yesteryear, I could hear she felt trapped; like there was no other place to go and no other people to be with. She'd make toasted sandwiches and lemonade and tell us stories to make us smile. With fellow feeling, she'd deflect from me, if not absorb, Andy's daggers of cruelty. She proved to be a lifesaver, as well.

Sheila could see Andy was rapt in rage as he drove the barrel of his gun into the hinge of my jaw. Easily twenty pounds heavier, and measurably stronger, she jumped on his back like she was ready for a piggy-back ride. With her arms wrapped high and clasped around his neck, with one hard yank, she pulled his head back with all her might, choking him and bringing him to the ground. The reversal snapped Andy out of his murderous mania. Thank God.

Gathering himself, he laid his gun on the table and, in Bronson-esque fashion, lit a cigarette. Eyes and jaw set, heaving and sweating, as if he'd just fought off an entire street gang, he proceeded to stare Sheila down and then me. He was reaffirming to himself, as much to us, that he was still in control.

"You listen to me real good, man." He leaned in on me.

With the hand holding his cigarette, he pointed his bony, resined, nic-stained fingers at my eyes, intentionally bringing the cherry of his smoke close to my face. "You're gonna pay me every last cent."

He leaned back drained, never moving his threatening eyes from mine.

"Don't even come around here 'til you have my money. Ya hear?" he huffed through curls of smoke. "And … if I find out … that you're cuttin' me out, man, I'm gonna kill you. You remember that."

"I will! I promise I will."

He stood up fast like he suddenly remembered he had someplace to be.

"Talk is for losers and fools, boy! Losers and fools." (He was a die-hard Eagles fan.)

Glaring down at me, he picked up his gun and lodged it in his belt behind his back. Raising his boot as high as he could, he brought it down hard, dead center on the little glass coffee table.

Crash! Demolished.

I dodged, scattering glass and mangled aluminum at eye level. Still trapped in that insufferable beanbag chair.

"Now, get the hell outta my house!" he screamed with vicious volume and blustered a half lunge at me, as though he was going to punch me again. His entire body was quivering with fury.

I watched the most dangerous man in my world stagger out of the room. I have no doubt it was by the mercies of God I was not killed. I'm forever thankful.

Dead Man Walking

The next few months, day after day, hour by hour, click by click, the pirate relentlessly ratcheted up my worry to anxiety to dread; my fears to panic to paranoia; my grief to oppression to depression. I was barely functional, a dead man walking. Under a reign of terror and duress, the bull ring had been violently and satisfactorily lodged into my nose.

Every thought was filtered through *what if. What if* my parents knew? *What if* Andy comes after me? *What if* someone was watching me? *What if* the police were coming for me? *What if* someone hurts my family? *What if* I couldn't get the money? The list was endless.

Everything I ate was tasteless. Sleep was impossible, making school, basketball, running, everything, miserable. I couldn't trust anyone because, you know, liars and deceivers think everyone else is lying, too. Nor could I tell anyone what had happened to me. I had no idea how to ask for help.

My life had been swallowed whole by the gun-drawn threats of a crazed candyman and an eye-to-eye standoff with the reaper. Like a sledgehammer driving a railroad spike, probably a thousand times a day, the pirate would pound the thought deeper and deeper into my soul: *You've ruined everything.*

I could not begin to imagine my life would ever be good again. I'm humbled to tell you that I began to think of how I could end my life.

I was in the middle of this raging river, imagining how to end my life, before I even realized where I was. I woke up to baleful thoughts before I recognized what they were or from whom they'd come.

I wrote a dozen suicide notes to my family—thank-yous, memories, apologies. By God's grace, I never delivered any of them. I tried to picture what my home and church, my basketball team and my school, would be like if I bowed out. I envisioned the heartbreak of my parents and the embarrassment I would cause my siblings. I thank God I didn't arrive at a detailed plan.

Miracle Move

My dad poked his head inside my bedroom door. "We're movin'," he announced calmly and matter-of-factly. "To Louisiana."

"What?" Surprised.

"Why?" Intrigued.

"Where?" Hopeful.

"When?" Excited.

"Papa's church, in Shreveport, needs a music director. So, we're going. It'll be a few weeks."

I remember where I was standing, what I was wearing, and the smell of the candle burning in my room when my dad delivered that news. By the hand of God, my father had walked into my pitch-dark world, turned on a flashlight, and showed me a doorway leading out into the sunshine.

I'm thankful for the decision he and my mother made to move our family; it likely saved my life. Words can't adequately convey the relief, the joy, and the resurgence of hope I tasted. It was as though my dad had secured his own oxygen mask and then mine. In a moment, the tonnage of fear and woe I was dragging rolled off. I could breathe.

My family arrived in Shreveport, Louisiana, eight days before I began my senior year of high school.

I've often wondered if the security guard ever told my parents, coaches, or anyone else, for that matter, about my foolishness and his gracious reprieve. No one said anything to me. No one, except the pirate, that is.

"You're mine," he routinely whispered. "Never forget that."

UNDER ANOTHER FLAG

Thunderstruck, the crew discovers themselves hijacked in unfamiliar waters. The only life they've known is dutiful and orderly service to their captain. For the pirates, though, these are waters for which they've been bred in the bone. Chaos, violence, and shame all contribute to an atmosphere of impending doom. Subjugation is their turf. Brute force is their native air.

Sailing for West Texas

You may think staring death in the eyes and agonizing under the flag of dire threats solved my drug and alcohol problems. It didn't. I wish I could tell you moving to a new city had given me a fresh start. I had, indeed, left Riverside, but the pirate hadn't left my ship.

Within hours of my family pulling in to Shreveport, Louisiana, before our boxes were even unpacked, my brother and I were invited to a party.

"How?" you may ask. Pirates attract pirates. We were promptly intertwined with two of the most active drug channels in the area. Ken, my older brother, had enough sense not to carry substances for any dealers.

Me? My soul required acceptance and friends in this new place, not to mention I had addictions that still needed to be looked after.

With most of my crew—my gifts, talents, and dreams—well under the pirate's rule, he double downed on his efforts to refit my ship for his use. By the time I graduated from high school, in May 1982, I had become someone I couldn't recognize. Under the flags of addictions, fears, and pride, I ended my senior year as one of my school's primary sources for coke, smoke, weed, and speed.

80

A few weeks after I walked across the platform with my class of '82, shook the principal's hand, and received my diploma, Ken and I set sail for West Texas.

Hired by a family friend, we were moving to San Angelo to join a management team opening up a retail store. We had three days before we were to present ourselves to the higher-ups for our new positions. From Shreveport to our new digs, near the Concho River, was only a seven-hour trip. We nearly didn't make it.

Tycoon's

"Rack 'em up!" bellowed the biker from beneath his onerous tobacco-stained beard, slamming his beer mug onto the long oak bar. Sighing with boondocks boredom, the large and densely tatted man snagged his pool cue like it was the neck of a chicken.

"Pleasure," Ken replied in his best Patrick Swayze impersonation, with a nod of suave toward me I had come to appreciate.

We had turned into a frontage road dive, killed the headlights of Ken's '73 Oldsmobile Cutlass, and coasted across the gravel lot, coming to rest in front of a poorly lit sign: *Win billiards, win beer!*

"Looks like our kind of spot," Ken intoned nonchalantly.

"I don't know, man," I warned from my usual perch of apprehension if not straight-up fear. "It looks pretty dim."

"I'm hungry. We win billiards, we win beer." Ken stepped out and slammed the unbalanced car door, leaving me to make up my mind in silence.

I trailed him up the ramp and into Tycoon's, a dilapidated trailer house on the outside, modified to look like a Texas saloon on the inside. With its towing hitch as much a permanent fixture as the concrete plinths it rested on, the bar was a *far piece* removed from any semblance of its name. We crept in pre-defined by our glaring differences.

Born and raised in Southern California, Ken and I had not yet acclimated to southern attire or music. We intruded on the countryfied atmosphere wearing OP shorts and tank tops.

"Fellas?" We were welcomed suspiciously, more like wondered at, by the weathered barkeep-slash-fryer and by drowsy chin dips from a few locals roosting at a card table.

"What're y'all havin'?" he asked, competing with the banjo and harmonica duet crackling from an old stereo cabinet. He never looked up from the rag he was dragging tiredly across the bar.

"Two cheeseburgers and two beers, please. Can we shoot for the beers?" Ken never missed a turn to make a dollar or avoid spending one.

"You'll have to put up for the beers 'fore ya play. If you take the table, I'll put it on your burgers; if not, well, ya already paid."

"Okay, sounds good." Ken spun boyishly on one of the stools and leaned his elbows onto the bar as he slapped down a handful of dollars. "Who'm I playin'?"

He scooped a handful of roasted peanuts from the glass Texaco ashtray and scanned the small room as he threw a few nuts into his mouth.

"That'd be me." One of the biggest men I've ever seen in my life stood up at the far end of the trailer, causing the entire structure to creak and roll as if from a small tremor.

Wheezing and grunting, he shoved chairs and tables to the side as he lumbered to the other end of the shaking room to the single pool table. He wore a Harley vest I could have used for a bedspread, with enough chain to braid a fence.

"Rack 'em up!" Due to the tall cone shape his leather bandana made on the top of his head and the tininess of the room, he appeared even more massive than he was. His enormity filled the smoke-steeped rickety trailer.

"Pleasure." Ken wiped his hands on his ragged corduroy shorts and pushed off of the bar. Gliding toward the pool table, he brushed the plastic triangle from its nail and caught it midair, shooting me a glance only he and I would understand.

Oh no. Here we go.

Now, I wouldn't say Ken was a pool shark, but he'd do until a real one came along. He could run the table eight times out of ten. I was a decent player but can't boast of ever beating Ken—not one game.

Fact is, I never knew Ken to lose a game of pool except by design. I watched him play with warped firewood and beat men who'd gleefully stared him down while delicately threading their maple-and-abalone-handled cues together.

Had my brother grown up in the 1800s, he would have been a Doc Holliday type, frail and weak, smart as a whip, and a hustler. He combined his acquired knowledge of angles, his innate charm, and his passion to make money by pretense, to effectively con many an unsuspecting fish. Ken was a brilliant actor.

At four years old, he and my folks discovered he had juvenile diabetes and would likely live only a few years. He decided he'd make the best life possible with what he had. He couldn't outrun you on the football field or take you down on a wrestling mat but had resolved early in his journey that he'd find ways to win.

Like Doc, he had the quickest draw of wit of anyone I've ever known. He had five jokes, two quotes, and three anecdotes for any situation. He was never at a loss for words—mostly humorous, often dangerous, always entertaining.

He and I had both been married for several years when, during one of our late-evening phone calls, he confessed, "I knew I wouldn't die as a kid. God decided that I would live."

He went to heaven in the winter of 2007.

During that late-night pool hustle at Tycoon's, somewhere in the middle of the Texas countryside, we were thinking about a lot of things, but God wasn't among them. Ken took the stage.

"Nah, that ain't right." Goliath flashed a silver eyetooth, grinning his complaint. "The yella ball goes on the top," he schooled through slurred speech, already on the tipsy side of his evening.

"Here?" Ken fumbled the balls, making them roll all helter-skelter across the table as though he was a novice. "Like this?"

I snicker-grinned, sitting eye to eye with a stuffed armadillo posed with a yellow-back coral snake hanging out of its mouth.

We'd grown up without a television or video games, and our parents were youth pastors. Shooting pool was our life. We had a table in our garage and full access to the one in the college student center, and we enjoyed a fairly decent table in our church fellowship hall.

We had both played a lot of pool. Ken could be counted on for an impromptu performance of any number of trick shots. He could sink any ball while awkwardly holding a crooked cue, portraying himself as one who was "lucky" and had no clue as to what he was doing. This was one of the essential skills of his schtick.

"You're pretty good!" Ken praised his prey, who had won the first game. "I guess your beer is on me. Go again?"

"Rrrack 'em up!" The bear-like guzzler belched.

"Well, if you don't mind," Ken articulated with pristine clarity, "since you beat me out of my beer, how about this time we play for two beers? That way, if I win, I can cover one for my brother, as well. Ya good with that?"

"Yup," he grunted, convinced there was no way he could lose.

Like the smoke of the men's cigars, the intensity had reached a hazardous level and had spread to the little huddle of cowboys now studying every move my brother and I made.

Ken dumped the first two games but went on to win the next three. That wasn't exactly the problem. After he tanked the second game, Ken, as was his routine, had convinced his fish to "freeze a fifty." (Players can't quit until one wins fifty dollars.)

At some point of ease, unaware, Ken dropped his act. On the fifth game, the novice ran the table. The sizeable soft touch didn't get one shot. Exasperated, he moved very slowly, as though he was doing all he could to keep from coming unhinged. Coldly, he peeled a fifty-dollar bill from his roll of cash and laid it gently in the center of the pool table.

It had become evident to everyone that Ken couldn't be beaten any more than the snake in the stuffed state animal's mouth would actually be eaten. It had all been for show.

"You boys better get now, while the gettin's good," the gaffer urged, clearing away our dirty dishes. "Tyc don't like to lose, 'specially in his own place. And that's fer sure."

No sooner had we been warned when Tyc, the proprietor of Tycoon's and, unbeknownst to us at the time, the prince of pool in the area, slammed his cue down across the short rail, breaking it in half and shooting splinters in every direction.

He was drunk.

He was livid.

We were in trouble!

Ken looked like a choirboy whose face had frozen while singing the word *Oh!*

Flashing eyes, heightened brows, and hands motioning as though he were throwing a bucket of dirt over his shoulder, Ken screamed at me, "Let's go! Let's go!"

We bolted for the door.

Ken struggled to turn the small beat-up aluminum knob; it was jammed.

Plaash! A heaved whiskey bottle crashed into the Coors Lite clock just above my head. Glass from the clock face felt like warm ants as it rained down onto my head and hunched shoulders.

I saw Tyc bend down and reach for something beneath the pool table. I cussed forcefully, imagining the worst!

I pushed Ken out of the way and got ahold of that flimsy doorknob. With double-fisted, fear-for-my-life adrenaline, I cracked it back and forth until it broke open.

Ken first, then me, at breakneck speed, vaulted over the railing of the ramp, landing on either side of Tyc's Harley, a massive green and white shovelhead bagger with a personalized plate: *Lil Tyc.*

For an intoxicated big man, Tyc moved fast. He was already out of the door, shouting and stumbling headlong down the wet ramp. To our advantage, it had been raining.

"We don't appreciate cheaters in these parts!" he seethed, brandishing his sword-like pool cue. "We shoot ringers 'round here!"

Ken, pedal to the metal, fishtailed out of the parking lot, sending gravel flying toward the trailer, Tyc, his Harley, and the locals. I heard the pebbles bouncing off of their trucks. I was gripped with panic.

Here we are again. We've signed our own death warrants!

"Yeehaaaw!" Ken wailed.

He was laughing hysterically and just roaring with delight. In his mind, we had gotten away with all of it. We were safe, sure as shootin'. I wasn't convinced.

I hung over the front seat gaping out of the rear window. I watched all the regulars, gathered at the door and waving their fists, shrinking in the growing distance. I was frantically searching for any clues that we were being chased.

All I could see was the dim and fading light of the small Tycoon's sign. Then, headlights swiftly swung onto the road.

"They're coming." I could barely breathe the words. My imagination was going haywire, flying at me with all Tyc and his crew would do to us if they caught us. "They're coming after us, Ken!"

"Don't worry! Don't worry," he insisted. "We're fine."

"Why? Why did you run the table?" I pleaded for an explanation.

"It's fun!" He laughed freely, still honking the horn and swerving the car.

"This isn't fun!" I scolded my elder brother as I took hold of the front dash with both hands. "This ain't even close to fun!"

We made it back to the highway, keeping our getaway speed. We were well down the road before I looked back again.

"I think we've lost 'em." I sighed with relief.

"Well, we didn't have to pay for our beer!" Ken smiled, cranking up the volume on the radio.

Up in Smoke

Exhausted but excited, we dragged into the quiet streets of San Angelo in the amber glow of Sunday morning's sunrise. It felt like the college town was on life support. On weekends, its engines didn't even rev until midmorning, and then only about half voltage.

Ken pushed open the door to the apartment one of our store managers had pre-rented for us.

"Oh, man! Whoa!" Ken quickly backed out of the door slamming into me. "Sorry, I thought this was ..."

"Hey! Hey! It's okay. Come on in! Kevin? Art?"

"Yeah. No. No. Ken. Ken is my name. Who are you?"

"I'm Danny." The tall and gangly one introduced himself, looking down at us, waving pot smoke away from his scraggly-bearded face. He looked like a tree without any leaves.

"Ken, huh? I thought yer name was Kevin. Well, good ta meetch y'all."

"I'm Billy." The much shorter and shy one whispered, shifting a joint to his other hand, so as to offer his handshake to Ken. "Glad to meet you."

On the top, he wore a bright-orange tractor cap, buried so low on his head, his eyes were completely hidden. On the bottom, curled up and pointy, mud-caked, high-heeled boots granted him a generous half inch.

"We knew y'all was comin' ta-day but not 'til later on." Danny, in his West Texas genteel, aimed to calm our obvious startle. "Y'all made it in early."

We had received a key and an address in the mail, along with a note of welcome from our store manager. It surprised us to discover two strangers, also employed by the store for its opening, would be our roommates. It was awkward.

We learned that Danny worked for Ken in soft lines and Billy worked for me in the warehouse. I don't know who arranged it, but because Ken and I were in management, we each had our own bedroom. Our roomies bunked in the common room on a couch and a recliner.

Adding to the strangeness of the relationship, they were both a few years older than we were and had already been working at the store for several weeks before we arrived.

It felt unsettling, like the angst of lighting a short fuse, when we watched them remove their belongings from the bedrooms and relocate to the living room. They seemed okay with it, but the pride of four males, cooped up in a two-bedroom apartment, can only hold out so long.

Danny and Billy were just like us, in all the wrong ways. Drugs and drink dominated every strand of their lives. They were heavy smokers and dipped Skoal and Copenhagen. Every crevice and surface of my life was saturated with smoke, either of cigarettes or marijuana; and spit cups, bottles, or whatever these brutes could find to spit their tobacco in. Our apartment wasn't cluttered or bachelorishly unclean; it was a declared disaster area! Noxious.

Overused and underwashed clothes, soured towels, and empty containers of whatever were strewn around from top to bottom. Spoiled food and dirty dishes were everywhere except the kitchen sink. And the smell? Beyond belief! I had never lived like this.

I was raised with the daily responsibilities of chores, everyone contributing to the quality of conditions. We didn't have a lot, but what my family did have, we kept clean and orderly. Along with structure, my parents had instilled in us a dignity that included the value of property and the quality of life.

Sadly, Ken and I had abandoned our prided disciplines for deliberate dysfunction the first chance we got. This was a keen faction of the pirate's agenda of depredation in my life. He would show me how low he could bring my existence, all with my full cooperation.

One night, around 10:00 p.m., after an extended shift, I came home famished. I wanted to eat a sandwich or two and relax for a few minutes before getting some sleep.

Shouldering through the half-opened front door of our beleaguered apartment, I stepped into what felt like an opium den. There were six or seven people, all of whom I had never met, sprawling around in different stages of stupor. They'd been drinking, snorting, smoking hash, and were now mostly sleeping to an eight-track of Boston.

For a split second, the real me took a peek behind the curtain. I knew right then *I am too far from home.*

I grimaced with anger and shame as I navigated trash, bodies, fog, and disjointed furniture.

What am I doing?

My heart sank. I was longing for the comforting lights of my father's house.

I don't belong here.

In no way did our squalor keep out the squatters. On any given night, in addition to us, the four rent payers, there were two to five rounders who couldn't make it home and took the liberty of just passing out somewhere in the crash pad.

I opened the refrigerator and found two cases of beer, a jar of pickle juice (all the pickles had been eaten, but no one made an effort to throw the jar away), a half-wrapped block of moldy cheese, an expired package of putrefied lunch meat, three rolls of Skoal cans, and three rolls of Copenhagen. Oh, and an industrial-size container of French's mustard.

Our cupboards were equally empty: half of a loaf of stale bread, an empty box, at one time promising strawberry Pop-Tarts, a leaking spray bottle of 409, and an abundance of water bugs and cockroaches.

The lights in my soul flickered on for just a moment. An empty me stared into the empty fridge.

Plenty of beer but no food.

An apartment that's full of people, but I'm deeply alone.

Pockets full of money but an empty pantry.
This is where I live.
This is what I've allowed myself to become.

It didn't change anything, but I remember thinking about it. Maybe it was a seed sown by Grace. I went to bed hungry.

In the midst of my mess, Love refused to let me go. Tenaciously tuned in to the activities of the pirate and I, God, would wrestle with me in His mercy. For instance, two blocks away from my bedroom window was a Lutheran Church that boldly rang its tower bells throughout the day and offered one soft chime at midnight, the bolder to give fair warning, the softer to afford a warm reminder.

Many nights, God used this single, barely audible chime to prick my heart. With my head pillowed, swirling but silent from the outside world, He would tell me He loved me.

"You say the Word, Arthur," He vowed, "and I'll put the pirate on the run!"

I rejected His offer more times than I can remember.

Have you ever seen a kid jump onto a motorcycle for the first time thinking, *How hard can this be?* He knows how to drop it into first gear, so he's convinced he can manage it.

He turns the accelerator and things begin to happen; too fast. His untrained mind, hands, and feet can't react quickly enough and the bike, out of his control, drives him into a light pole, or worse?

That was me setting out to manage a warehouse team of twenty-two people. I had never done anything like it before.

How hard can this be?

It became a certified disaster.

I made $1,400 a month. My monthly bills were $300. That was a lot of money and a lot of capitalized clout for an eighteen-year-old kid who had never lived away from his parents. It almost killed me.

I bought clothes and a car, stereos, and a lot of pointless possesions. Mostly, I bought drugs and booze. I opened a checking account so I could cash my check. I scarcely deposited money into it and never edged it above $400. I spent all I had. My life had swiftly saddled onto the script of the old stoner movie, *Up in Smoke.*

I'm a paragon of the Prodigal. I had a beautiful family and, in my estimation, an exceptional rearing. I willingly, and wantingly, left everything and sailed away on my own. When the pirate took control of my ship, my crew—my gifts and talents, dreams, and desires—converted to selfish ambitions, wantonness, and destructive living. My passions and few convictions were overwhelmed and thrown overboard.

In all of my thrashing about, like a fish out of water, one night left a mark on my heart that will forever be there.

A Rooster's Crow

"You gotta be there, Art! It's gonna be the party everybody's talkin' about, man!" Steve, a warehouse employee, gushed. A few years older than me, he lived with his affluent jet-setting parents. "You definitely can't miss this!"

"Yeah, okay, sounds good." I smiled sheepishly. I was still painfully uncomfortable at parties—at any gatherings, for that matter. "Thanks, Steve."

Always mindful of my *p*'s and *q*'s, I was already sick to my stomach with worry. The pirates of fear, rejection, and self-loathing allied on the deck of my ship and promptly began their threatening and mockery. I couldn't silence them.

"What a place!" I gawked. Ken and I pseudo-sauntered past the long row of foot lamps, through the aisle formed by two Porches and a Shelby Mustang, toward the arched entryway of the mansion.

The front porch of Steve's Tudor house was cathedral-like, bigger than our apartment and with its own swaggering chandelier. I could hardly believe I'd been invited to such a place. Inside were more than a hundred of the most beautiful and wealthy people I'd ever seen, let alone mingled with.

Hey, look at you, man. You're doin' all right.

Once again, I mistakenly took my role—a drug-using, drug-carrying young manager with spare change and access to the regional manager's ear—as actual acceptance. I was in way over my head.

"This is for you, sir." A waiter, wearing a black Peak Lapel tuxedo, handed me a cocktail from his tray. I couldn't help but stare. This was a first for me.

"And, for your pleasure," he further offered, gracefully motioning with his white-gloved hand, "inside the blue door, just there, are complimentary cocoa and leaves." (I had to go inside the blue door to find out what he was talking about. These are terms used in high society to refer to cocaine and marijuana.)

"Hello, Art! I'm Jerry!" He lodged his cigar between his teeth and shot me his thick, overly bedecked hand. "I'm Steve's father!"

He dressed and spoke over-the-top, like an intransigent politician who needed to be seen and heard by everyone. "I'm glad you came! I've heard a lot about you!"

I put my hand in his and almost went to my knees as he crushed bone to bone.

"Hello, sir." I winced. "Thank you. I'm glad to—"

"Call me, Jerry!" He blustered, vise-gripping my shoulder with his free hand. "Please, you're in my home. Call me Jerry!"

I pried my hand free from his clutch of control.

"This is a very nice home you—"

"Oh, thank you! Thank you! I'm glad that you like it! It's …"— long inhale, with that legend-in-his-own-mind-cameras-are-rolling kind of gaze—" …the smallest of our three."

He gusted his cotton-candy-sweet cigar smoke, making zero effort to avoid my face. "I hope that you'll visit us in Rome when you have the chance." He made a quick scan of the room to be sure he'd hijacked everyone's attention.

"Anyway, Ken? He's your brother?!"

"Yes, sir, Ken is my—"

"Yeah, grrreat guy! He's a smart one, that one! He told me that your folks are pastors in a church. Pastors? Is that right?!"

I would have handed over every dollar in my pocket for an escape hatch beneath the Persian Qum rug beneath us.

"Well, they're not pastors. But, yeah, they're ministers …" My effort to lower the volume of our one-sided conversation was unsuccessful.

"Well, that's just precious!" he shouted as he raised his glass and twirled to face the crowd. "Isn't that precious, everybody?!"

People clinked their glasses together like they were toasting my adorableness. It felt like everyone there had been hypnotized, brought under (or bought under) Jerry's ascendency. There wasn't an original among them.

"Yeah! That's precious!" someone echoed.

"Aww! That's so sweet," someone else cooed in a high, condescending voice.

I gaped at my feet, avoiding eye contact with anyone.

"You know what you call a preacher's kid, don't cha', Art?!" Jerry sang.

I simpered.

"A parolee-ee!" He, the lead, with a hundred backup mockers, laughed ludicrously.

It kicked up buried pain from fourth grade. On the playground, I was surrounded by what seemed to be the whole school. For the pleasure of the cheering crowd, a few sixth-grade strong arms had stuffed my own Twinkie up my nose and into my ears. Grade-school antics, I know, but soul throttling.

Growing up in a minister's home, I had sustained plenty of bullying; being ridiculed by a jury of adults was a new experience. As was my inclination, I was overly sensitive and took it hard. The pack of wolves had sniffed out my mutinous insecurities.

"No, seriously now, Art! What about you?" Jerry wryly egged on, both barrels blazing. "Are you a preacher or a parolee?!"

His perceptive wife floated to his side and gently laid her hand inside the crook of his elbow. Discerning my agony, she tried to rein him in.

"Well, I—"

"Are you a believer? Hah! Hah!" He emphasized the word *believer* for special attention as he continued to gambol in his dominance over the enclosing pack and me. "Are you one of *those* Christians?!"

Though not the pirate, Jerry expressed the enemy's cruelty and tyrannical spirit decisively.

"No!" I blurted out, fighting for a chance to say something, anything. I was startled and heartsick to hear the words fall out of my mouth.

"I'm not a preacher. I don't even believe in God," I draggled.

Jerry stood hushed in a long, victorious pause. Like a prosecuting attorney, having satisfactorily put the accused in his place, glares in silence, waiting for the gravity of his triumph to land. Then, when all of the oxygen has been sucked out of the room, he smirks. "The people rest, Your Honor."

Staring at me, if not studying me, through thick cigar smoke rising in sinister swirls to veil his squinting eyes, he finally spoke, low and slow with a grand crescendo, "Well, I guess that makes you a parolee, then!"

His guest roared in amused approval, a contrived chorus, like manipulated minions.

"Hah! Hah! Hey, everybody, we've got a convict on the run!"

He was right, one way or another.

Later I learned Jerry hated Christians in general, and this had been a calculated attack, a sophisticated siege.

Bored by the fizzled firecracker, everyone went back to other conversations. Jerry slowly raised his drink to my face, downed the liquor in a gulp, then slammed his Z-stem martini glass onto the marble countertop.

He was disappointed I hadn't been a more worthy opponent. The kingpin took his silent wife by the arm and led her to others who were waiting for their company.

The bully left and had left his mark.

The pirate sneered, taunting my weakness; my cowardice. For his intents and purposes, he had refit and renamed my ship, converted or killed all of my crew, and now, he had victoriously raised his flag over my life. The Oppressor overshadowed everything.

A bird of flight eventually gives way to gravity. I folded under the pull of the enemy's strongholds of addictions, shame, and fear, and the newest grapple hook, castigation.

Annihilated and all but disembodied, I preened in the shadows of that impressive room the best I could. Gasping and grappling for some thread of composure, I struggled to recover from the shock and awe of the last three minutes.

I guzzled the booze and spent way too much of the rest of the night on the wrong side of the blue door. It was wall-to-wall with dangerous people who were much higher than I'd ever been.

I'm almost sure I heard a rooster crow.

Doomed

Ken had left Steve's party around midnight, leaving me to slosh home alone. I have no memory of the trip. I give thanks to God for allowing me to find my bed.

Lying down in the darkness and silence, I turned my face to the side and pulled my pillow underneath my head. Just before sleep came, I saw the dim light of my digital clock roll over to 3:00 a.m., needling another barb just under my skin.

On a warm summer night under the light of a high moon, with a flashlight firmly pressed to the bottom of his chin, shining upward to deform his face, a childhood friend had warned me, "Three in the morning is the witchin' hour, man! Always, always be asleep by then!"

I never believed it mattered, but the warning and the image lodged themselves in my soul for years.

Like a convicted criminal waiting for his pending due, I laid in the deafening silence, staring at the clock rehearsing and weighing what I had done.

Am I a Judas? I'm a Judas.

Am I a Peter? They both denied Jesus, but one of them was forgiven?

Oh, God, can You ever forgive me?

I just couldn't believe it. If I would've known how I could have shifted my fear of penalty over to faith in God's mercy. I didn't have the understanding. You can imagine how the Accuser took advantage of my fragmented soul and ruptured heart.

The Bible says God can't forgive you, the pirate jeered. *You're finished!*

My perceptions, naturally and spiritually, were demolished. Eighteen years old, drunk, stoned, dismantled, having just publicly denied even knowing God, lying in my bed at 3:00 a.m., far away from my father and my mother.

I imagined an angry-faced God, pointing His long, judgmental finger to a place beyond me and away from Him, a place of eternal darkness. The precious truths and promises I once held of God's plan for my life were all slipping away from me like precious grains of sand through my aching and weakening fingers.

Satan, unremittingly, landed his blows.
You've committed the unpardonable sin.
That's what you've done, you coward.
There is no place for you now!"
Relentless.

There's a term druggies use to describe the impending crash that slams hard, soon after being so high: *wasted*. This is how I felt about my young life; it was wasted. Blinded by the Spirit of Deception, it seemed everyone I loved and everything I cared about had been ripped away. Any flag of God's, or my own—honor, purpose, peace, love, joy, all of them—had been buried beneath fear, shame, and rejection.

I thought I was in control.

I thought I could navigate and negotiate with the pirate.

I thought I had welcomed a friend on board.

Now, here he had, *we had*, reduced my life to rubble.

I didn't mean it, God! Please forgive me. I didn't mean what I said.

I pleaded in sincere conviction and contrition.

I'm a Judas.

I betrayed Jesus.

God can't forgive me.

Doomed.

I hadn't meant it any more than Peter had when he denied knowing Jesus. But I remembered being taught, and with naïvety had construed it as a threat, *If you deny Jesus before men, He'll deny you before His Father in Heaven.*

Steeping in accusation, worry, stupor, and loneliness, I fell asleep to the murmurings of the pirate. "I'm going to kill you."

MANIFEST

The witting hijacker knows, where there's no manifest, no vision or direction, the ship will perish. The pirate's chief aim in destroying your ship's manifest is to cause you to throw off restraint, lose your direction and purpose, and spend the rest of your days wondering and wandering, listlessly, in the open seas of life, vulnerable to the whims of any and all pirates.

Oh no! I blinked at the clock in disbelief.

It couldn't be 6:15 a.m.! I was supposed to be there at five.

I'm gonna be fired!

This wasn't the first time I'd overslept.

Though my manifest had been shredded and my rudder disabled, I was yet convinced I was in control; I could navigate this. I had crossed the midnight hour, carousing into the early morning until collapsing on my pillow around two thirty.

Just a couple of hours is all I need, I had assured myself.

When I finally made it to the store, at 6:45, the parking lot looked like a hamlet of tiny cottages with fires aglow through their ice-frosted windows. In fact, each little hut was a truck or car, where my warehouse employees huddled around their heaters and had been waiting, some since as early as 4:45, for my arrival. I had the keys to the store.

"I'm an idiot! I know it," I blubbered smarmily, navigating through a huddled handful who had decided to light up and wait it out on the loading dock. "I apologize. Don't shoot me! I'm so sorry. I oversl—"

"No mystery here, Mr. Evans. No need to explain anything!" Mr. Adams mumbled into his chilled cupped hands. "We all know how this goes."

Cocooned in his Marlboro Man fleece jacket, the puffy cloud of the retired rancher's warm breath accentuated my irresponsibility and selfishness toward these precious people.

"Are we getting paid for sittin' out here the last hour or so?" Alice, a second-year college student wondered for everyone. She pulled down hard on the pom-poms dangling on either side of her head from her dead-leaves-brown knit cap. "The time clock won't punch the right time, ya know. Can you fix that for us?"

"Yes. I'll fix it." Frantic and panicking, I finally located the keys deep in my jacket pocket. "You'll be paid. I'm so sorry for making you guys have to wait!"

Cold, shaking, blurred by the booze binge, and aching with embarrassment, I struggled far too long in opening the enormous and sluggish roll-up dock door.

Klack-aack-aack! The heavy metal door complained every inch of the way up as it crawled rhythmically into its overhead cage. Undermining the anticipated comfort of being warmed, a dreadful, burn-your-eyes stench smothered us as we pressed into the warehouse.

Someone had left a coffee pot on overnight, cooking and caking the carafe with scorched tar. Likewise, my embarrassment was blistering as the exasperated crew of twenty or so broiled in their fitting frustration with me.

Shedding our layers of coats and sweaters, gloves and hats, murmurs and whispers were deliberately timed and toned to ensure I heard them. The barbs and jabs that pierced the most were those with a point of truth.

"I don't think this feller can do it! This is jus' too much for 'im."

"I've worked for him for months. You can count on 'im ... to always be late!"

"This is it for me. I'll be talkin' to Mr. Davis this morning. He's gotta go!"

Due to my lateness, my unshakeable lassitude, and the fact I didn't have it in me to look anyone in the face, we skipped our regular morning meeting and went right to work.

Sullen, I snatched my clipboard and hurried into the big house where dozens of iron-framed stacked storage bays, loaded with merchandise, framed every wall and reached to the top of the twenty-five-foot ceiling.

I fired off a few futile directives, hoping to relieve the awkwardness and reassert my credibility so we could work, at least, with some form of cooperation.

Gotta Get Up High

"Freddy! Gotta get up high, man!" I ordered, pumping my thumb in the air. "Swing your lift this way and put me on 14B!" I pointed to a third-level storage bay, where the hands-down best forklift driver in all of Texas had hoisted me many times.

We worked well together. About the same age, Freddy and I tended to cultivate a sense of adventure, if not risk, in this day-to-day task at the warehouse. Already on the move, he hit the gas on his lift and sped my way.

As if jumping onto a passing train, I landed on the fast-flying forks and took hold of one of the non-moving parts of the mast. With smooth synchronization, Freddy whisked me along toward bin 14 while raising the forks. The gust of cold wind in my face was refreshing.

You can imagine I looked like a pirate, hand on hip, searching the distant horizon while sailing at the top of my crow's nest, right down the middle of the warehouse. On a better day, you would have thought I owned the place.

Docking at 14B, I leaped on to the fifteen-foot-high pallet rack. I waved Freddy off. I planned to work at the site for some time. More like a boondoggle, really, a few moments away from everybody while I tried to gather myself.

Discouraged, disgusted, and distracted by my infraction, and gravely unrested, I overlooked, maybe ignored, a crucial protective measure: I didn't clip into the safety harness that was side-anchored into all of the storage bays above eight feet.

I was bending over with my head buried deep inside a house-sized box of towels. With my back toward the open edge of the storage rack, I was slogging through the cumbersome carton, unknowingly inching my back foot toward the ledge.

At last, after a long, body-stiffening, blood-rush-to-the-head stoop, I uncovered the packing form I'd been burrowing for. I raised up from the box, waved my prize over my head, and stepped backward—onto nothing.

Turn! Turn! Turn!

It's astonishing just how much detail your brain can process in the hundredths of seconds as you're falling, your life about to end.

First thought: *I am not ready to see God's face.*

Then, confusion. Panic. Dismay.

Oh, God! Help me!

I had the presence of mind to flip my body over so I could see to where, and to what, I was descending. Like blood-red, pulsating crosshairs, with one voice, my eyes, brain, heart, and every fiber within me screamed, *PALLET JACK!*

Barring intervention, my obituary would read: *Warehouse manager falls from fifteen-foot storage rack and is clotheslined by reinforced, solid steel 5,000 lb.-capacity pallet jack handle.*

Turn! Turn! Turn! My heart pleaded with my glaciated mind.

Desperately determined to do what was necessary, I flipped to my right side, avoiding the tall handle by a breath. I landed on my shoulder, elbow, head, and hip—thankfully, in that order. As if having a plan of its own to offer help of some kind, my right foot found a way to kick off its boot.

Flashes of light, distant stars, and bursts of colors danced and swirled on the dark canvas of my mind. Piercing heat, like the ends of one hundred soldering irons, melded my skull, my jaws, every bone and joint.

Why am I on the floor?

What happened?

How embarrassing.

Get up!

I tried to lift my head. I wanted to get up before anyone could see me.

Can you imagine? I wasn't thinking about the condition of my body, only the shame of being sprawled, seen immovable, confirmed as weak.

I couldn't lift my head, my legs, or my arms. Lying there on the concrete floor of the warehouse, I gave as forceful and repeated commands to my body as I knew how. Like an inanimate object, it refused me. The more I struggled, the more dizzy and nauseated I became. I threw up.

With everything on lock-down, the vomit pooled into my hair, ear, eye, and nose. I closed my eyes tightly, which felt like I was screw tightening a hose clamp around my forehead. I sank into a spin I couldn't escape.

Fading.

Darkness.

Heat.

Cold.

I'm Going to Kill You

" ... not moving?"

"He may be ..."

"What happened? Did he ..."

"Is he breathing? Is he moving? Can he move? He doesn't seem ... to ... be ..."

"He fell! Can you believe it?"

"He's been out like that for a long time."

"Too long!"

"From the top? That's gotta be fifteen, twenty feet!"

"He's dead! He's gotta be dead."

With strain, I commanded my eyes to open. One reluctantly forced itself, through muck and ooze of puke and blood, to open halfway. I smelled coffee; not the pleasurous aroma of fresh brew but the stench of coffee that had been forgotten and burnt.

I wouldn't remember what happened until many hours later. I wouldn't understand how I'd come to the ledge, to the brink of things, until many years later. Under the weight of dread, paralysis, and reality fighting to wriggle its way into my brain, suddenly, I remembered and shuddered as I rehearsed the haunting threat the pirate had exacted just days before: *I'm going to kill you!*

Please Come Home!

If you've ever been put under a deep anesthetic sleep, then you'll know what I mean when I say *in a blink* I was transported from the warehouse floor to a hospital bed. Obscure imaginings in between.

Quasi-awake, everything in low-grind gear, I was powerless to get my wheels turning. It's perplexing and unsettling to not be able to recall your name, what happened to you, or where you are in the moment. The room was dim, hazy, dull, and indistinct. It smelled like a bucket of fresh Clorox.

My right arm, in a kind of canvas sling, attached to the ceiling or something high, reposed in a waving goodbye position. Sedated, I lapsed in and out of dreamless and dream-rich sleep.

Even under a pile of blankets, I couldn't get warm. In shock and fighting for warmth, my body had the shivers that were more like violent shakes. They would begin in my shoulders and roll out of my feet.

I wished I was at home.

"Well, Mr. Evans, heard ya had a preeetty hard fall." The doctor responsible for my relief appeared out of nowhere and began digging through blankets to find my arm. His hands may as well have been blocks of ice.

"Can you feel this?" He pinched my left wrist, studying my face over the top of his gold readers.

"Yes," I whispered, surprised by the sound of my voice.

"Well, that's good!" He appeared genuinely relieved. "We hadn't got much outta ya 'til now."

He gently buried my arm beneath the covers and turned his attention to the beeping machines at the side of the bed. His head and courteous but concerned smile tilted to the side like he was gauging an experiment. After evaluating and fidgeting with the instruments for a while, he finally spoke.

"Ya know why ya here?" His lively way of talking paired well with his Wilford Brimley persona. His sentences would begin like a low breeze that quickly speeds up to a high gust. "Know what happ'm?"

"No, sir. I don't," I admitted anxiously, fully aware something had happened.

"Well, you fell at your work, from pretty high up, they tell me." He pushed his glasses up on his nose in rhythm for emphasis.

"You landed on your right elbow and shoulder … and your head." He placed his hand on his shoulder and then his head to be sure I was following him.

"You lost your breakfast and a couple of teeth, and that's about it … for your head. You're quite a miracle, ya know. Somebody must really be lookin' out for ya."

I nodded slowly, acknowledging but not quite convinced.

"Can't say the same 'bout chur arm." He leaned in extra close to my face and clicked on his penlight.

"You should feel this," he warned, shining his light into my right eye.

Oh, boy did I! The soldering iron made a comeback! Straight to the back of my skull. I winced, groaned, and slammed my eyes shut.

"Well, believe it or not, that's a good sign, too!" Measuring his smile, he kindly sought to see me over to the upside of things.

"You'll be back to normal in a bit." He stood up straight. "Well." He dipped his chin so his telling eyes could rise above his glasses and fix on mine. "That is, except for your arm."

"Pins, plates, grafts—none of that'll work. We're just gonna wrap ya up and letcha heal."

He stepped back, mindlessly clicking his penlight on and off, probably a reflexive fidget tempering him when delivering bad news.

"You won't be able to count on it much from here on out." He could tell I wasn't following what he was saying.

"I hope ya know how to use your left hand, cuz you'll never even write your name with the other. You've shattered it."

He returned his pen light to its spot in the overcrowded pocket of his bleach-white lab coat. He forced it in with several writing pens, bandage scissors, various sizes of cotton swabs, and other sundry tools.

"From your shoulder down to your wrist." He spread out all ten of his fingers toward me, showing me what he'd observed on my X-rays. "It looks like an up close map of a bunch of rivers, see?"

To my blank stare, he gave me the slightest smile and kind nod. Like the measured warmth given from a glowing fireplace when you've come in from the cold. It made me feel he understood that I was dealing with a lot.

"Okay, we'll check back with ya a bit later and getcha ready for the wrap. Your mother called earlier this afternoon." He stopped and turned at the door as though he had just remembered. "I assured her that I'd have you call her the moment you woke up."

"Afternoon?" I asked, rattled by being reminded of the concept of hours. "What time is it, please?"

The seasoned doctor, feeling my angst, picked up the phone from the right side of the bed and moved it to the other.

"It's almost five," he answered sympathetically. "You've had a long day."

"Hello?" Like the final blow of a mallet, the sound of her voice instantly fractured my levee of emotions. My soul was flooded, irrepressibly, once again, with embarrassment and fear, fear of what was happening and who was threatening my ship.

"Hi, Mom," I said through throaty tears.

"Hi, honey. Are you okay?" she asked with patented gracious intensity. "I knew something was wrong. I called you at the store this morning."

I felt her exhaustion from holding her own levee together during the silent hours she'd been waiting to hear from me; or from anyone on my end.

"Ken finally called me back and told me you'd been rushed to the hospital! What's going on? What happened?"

"I fell." I resisted the predictable efflux of information.

"Are you all right?"

"I'm fine," I answered, feeling sorry for myself. This was my mom, after all.

"Where? Where were you?" Four hundred and some odd miles away, she was anxious to get the full picture. "How'd you fall?"

"I'm not sure how it happened, mom," I answered truthfully, still cloudy on details. "I fell at work, in the warehouse. I broke my arm, hit my head, knocked out a couple of teeth. I'm pretty sore, but I'm gonna be fine."

I started to tell her what the doctor had said about never using my arm again. I crumbled in the middle of it and tearfully fizzled down to babble.

"I'm so sorry this happened, Art." She gently put her hope-filled shoulders under my burden. "I'm praying for you. Don't you think you should come home?"

She was urgently trying to catch my wind-whipped, frenzied kite string. She wisely restrained herself from confronting me with the many Scriptures flooding her heart.

All she heard from my end of the line was a deep, all-disclosing sigh.

"I love you, honey. Your dad and I are very concerned about you. Please come home. Okay? Please come home."

"I love you too, Mom. I better go." I hung up the phone and sobbed.

I Lost the Pathway to My Heart

What had happened to my life?

As a kid, I'd been kind, considerate, happy—very happy. Now, I felt like I'd stepped off solid ground and landed in a pit of quicksand. I was mean, irritated, annoyed, or downright angry all the time.

If I wasn't anesthetized by drink or drug, I was generally miserable. I was sinking by the minute with no help in sight. I'm not saying rope wasn't being offered, I just couldn't see it. Shame shadowed everything.

What had happened to my dreams?

I had childhood ambitions of playing in the NBA and traveling the world. I had even told one of my pastors I wanted to be a missionary to Russia. Now, I didn't care about anybody but myself and couldn't see anything past the white powder at the end of my nose.

Maybe you're thinking, *You should have known better, Art.*

I would agree with you. I did know better. Allowing the pirate to board my ship had not only cost me a great deal, it had drastically changed me.

When the Devourer of Dreams destroyed my manifest, annihilated along with it was my sense of my peace and purpose. I lost the pathway to my heart. I didn't know how to find the serene waters of sweetness anymore. It seemed everything in my life, from the inside out, was hard, cold, calloused, and crashing.

For the first time in my life, I felt hopelessly lost, to God, my parents, and to myself. I couldn't recognize myself and had no plumb line on who I was capable of becoming. It terrified me to my core.

This is one of the overarching reasons I know God can reach anybody: if He found me, my dear friend, He can find anyone.

He Lives Here

The next evening, while waiting for my discharge, Ken and I devoured bean and cheese burritos. As I told my brother all that had befallen me, it was as though I was telling someone else's story. Like a lousy photomontage of unfocused and unfamiliar images flying by, I couldn't yet hang on to what had happened.

"The doctor said you should likely be dead." Ken coolly reinforced my convictions, which were masquerading as confusion, that somehow God had mercifully intervened and saved my fouled-up life.

"He said, 'Your brother's a miracle!'" Ken chortled. "I said to him, 'Aren't we all?!'"

"Yeah, seriously. Aren't we all?"

Ordinarily, I admired his levity. But I wasn't in any humor to underplay the magnitude of what had occurred. Measuring the threats of the pirate—to my reality of the last thirty-five hours or so—brooding, I nodded indolently and forced one corner of my mouth up slightly.

I couldn't shake it.

I could have died, should have died.

How close I'd come.

"Well, you'd better get your act together, cuz I'm headed to Hattiesburg!"

"Whoa! What?" Bombshell! I had no idea this was even a possibility. "Why? When?"

He'd been reassigned to a management position with a store in Mississippi. We agreed the long-distance move had been determined because of the double-trouble effect. The fact was, the decision-makers got wise to what Ken and I had always known: we were both good workers, but together, we were unpredictable, if not dangerous.

He was my older brother by twenty-one months, but every new place we'd move to, most people thought we were twins; we didn't tell them otherwise. We'd go along with the idea, pretending and improvising whatever characteristics we could dream up.

One summer morning, Ken was inspired, inventive even. We were halfway through our first-of-the-season walk to the public swimming pool, where we'd spend long, sun-soaked days baking in the overly chlorinated soup of swimmers until our skin carbonized and our hair turned moldy green.

"How ... about ... you're ... deaf?" His hands were moving, spasmodically, in front of his face in what he thought was a good impersonation of sign language. We'd both observed it but hadn't the faintest idea how it worked.

"Huh?" I smiled, intrigued. "Whatdya mean?"

"Yeah!" Skipping a bit, his eyes flashed as his imagination sparked shivers of possibilities and an explosion of laughter. "You're deaf!"

The two-mile walk became script, rehearsal, and action for what we thought was to be a few minutes of fictional fun. We carried on the charade for the entire summer break, two and a half months!

Most were good-humored about it when, at long last, we abruptly revealed our sham. It was a dead giveaway when, one morning, right out of the blue, I began a conversation with Ken in perfect English.

A few, who Ken affectionately referred to as *buzzkills*, required a bit more explanation and hoped we would be sincerely remorseful for having dragged them through such an emotional experience.

"You guys are bad!" One of the bamboozled couldn't think of anything more to say.

Without pause, in his best Billy Gibbons, Ken sang, "We're nationwide!"

Remorseless, Ken and I flattered ourselves on our performances and moved on, searching for our next stage.

We had our share of knock-down drag-out fights, but we loved having each other around. While in church, or with my parents at someone's stuffy house, Ken and I communicated with signals, a secret vocabulary, and made-up languages no one else could understand.

As kids, our mischief was harmless and served to liven our mundane social obligations into grand adventures. Much more was at stake now.

We grew closer as friends when we moved from Riverside to Shreveport, and now to San Angelo. But like kerosene on a flame, we incited and emulated each other in all the wrong things. We weren't lifting each other higher, we were pulling each other down.

"I leave in two weeks." He brought me up to speed as he drove us to our apartment. "You're gonna be fine."

This news was the worst I could imagine. My body and, now my soul, throbbed in places where my heartbeat was fighting for life. The weight of my jacket became oppressive as I struggled for breath. I tried to regulate my inward pain by physically intensifying every provoking fissure in the road the tires of our car collided with. I was hollow inside, envisioning eating, sitting, and drinking alone. For the first time in our lives, we would live apart, and I would live on my own. I didn't navigate these new waters very well. I constricted a fist in my left hand until the spasms in my brachial muscle informed me that I had no more strength to grip.

Turning into our complex, Ken slowed the car to a crawl. We passed the empty swimming pool —except someone had thrown all of the vinyl-strap chairs into the bottom, forming a kind of groovy sculpture of neon green and faded yellow.

"Why are you going this way?" I asked, uncomfortable with anything out of the ordinary.

"Oh, I've got to show you somethin'!" He raised his head and eyebrows, staring down his nose at me with a you're-never-going-to-believe-this kind of smile.

He turned off the radio and eased the car around the end of our building, so slowly I could hear the pop of every piece of gravel. I couldn't imagine what was coming as he turned off the engine and coasted into a spot in the backlot, much farther from our door than he usually parked.

"What're we lookin' for?" I begged with equal amounts of fascination and fatigue.

"You'll see," he promised, softly lifting his door to close it as quietly as possible. "You're not even gonna believe it!"

We crept through the breezeway, as though we were playing hide-and-go-seek and trying to make it to home base without getting caught.

Oh, my gosh!

No way.

What's he doing here?

Reading my face and thoughts, Ken stood, shoulders pinned high to the wall, wide-eyed, with the biggest grin you can imagine. Both of his hands were across his chest with one finger pointing at the massive green-and-white shovelhead Harley. It had a personalized plate: *Lil Tyc.*

"He lives here," he whispered, bright-eyed, through his smug smirk.

We held our stare and our breath and sidled up the stairs to our apartment.

Teetering on a Tightrope

"Dude, don't cry!" Ken chided, slinging his last bag into the trunk and grabbing me in a headlock. "You're gonna be fine."

"Yeah, I'm sure I'll do fine." I wiped my eyes, hating where I lived even more. I dreaded the approaching holidays and the anticipating ache of loneliness.

"I sure wish you didn't have to go," I whined. "Be safe."

It was a bleak scene watching Ken drive off. He was on his way to Mississippi. I stood out on the road for the longest time, staring at the spot where his car had disappeared, sorely wishing I had packed it up and gone with him.

I'd been in San Angelo for six months and knew a lot of people. I didn't know anyone as a friend.

Like a bullet train flying through a tunnel, benumbed by Jim Beam and painkillers, I blew through the ridiculous retail rituals of December and January. Often late, always exhausted, and a spate of expensive-to-the-company bad decisions, I was a train wreck waiting to happen. I worked fourteen- and fifteen-hour blurred days, heavily fueled by cocaine or speed.

Oh, how I'd love to have had any of those precious wasted hours back. I've become immensely thankful for God's promise: "All the years the swarming locust, crawling locust, the consuming and chewing locust have devoured, I will restore to you."

For anyone who will put their past in His hands, God knows how to heal, deliver, and restore. All He needs is your invitation and trust.

I endured the next few months, strenuously mindful of the whereabouts of Lil Tyc at all times. Every morning as I left home, and each night when I returned before I dared to move, I'd scour the vicinity, hoping to not be seen.

Is he here?

Does he know that I live here?

Is he watching for me?

It was more fodder for the pirate.

When you travel with pirates, ease is a foreign concept. The close calls, the all-consuming chaos, and all the normal emotions in a blender of being eighteen had brought me to teetering on a tightrope.

On the one side, with obsessive surveillance and avoidance, I was navigating a suffocating paranoia of Tyc's potential pummeling and a fear that I could be fired from my job at any moment.

On the other side, with drugs and drink, I was mitigating sadness and feelings of rootlessness; I was heartsick for home. I was too immature to understand it at the time, but these were symptoms of a much broader condition.

I'd been severed from any and all anchors. I was drifting, powerless, and purposeless. I had no manifest, vision, or hopeful purpose to help guide my way.

Time to Go Home

Along with the patient persistence of my mom and dad, there was something else, or, someone else, fueling the drag on my heart toward the warm lights of home.

Just before Ken and I had set out for San Angelo, I had met a girl who, all the while I was in Texas, had written to me.

Long before we met, she had anchored her life in Jesus Christ. Her letters were full of light and joy. They would reach my heart with momentary effervescent beauty. Her words of kindness reminded me of God's goodness in my life in days gone by.

All the same, I had no confidence she'd have anything to do with me. All the time I'd survived in West Texas, steered by self-centered emptiness, I had only written her back once or twice.

In the nine short months of sailing on my own, the pirate had effectively shredded my ropes: my morals, convictions, and standards. With all his promises and prowess, I had allowed him, if not invited him, to board my ship. He had sailed full-steam ahead and gained access to every part of my life. The tyrant had successfully altered everything in how I perceived, understood, and navigated my world. In effect, he had reshaped my soul to think, talk, and carry out the captain's plans like a pirate.

In the wake of following his ways of doings and dealings, I was hanging on by the last thread. The pirate and I exchanged thoughts:

Why am I still living in this hellhole? I brooded.

Because you've got to make your own way!

I could feel his sharp, accusing finger thumping my chest.

That's what this is all about! He taunted. *Remember?!*

Yeah. But I could get a job in Shreveport, I reasoned. *I could be closer to my family.*

You could, he argued. *And that, of course, would be admitting you're a fool and a failure, a coward, that you don't have what it takes!*

Yeah? Well, look at me!

I nodded at the surroundings of my clogged and cluttered bedroom as confirmation.

That fact has already been made abundantly clear!

Yeah, well, this is just like you, man! You're a crybaby and a quitter. What a shame. I'm gonna take you out yet!

In early February, to the jubilation of my store's manager, I resigned from my position.

On Friday, the day after a nurse cut off the fiberglass cast from my arm, Beauty and I started our drive of shame back to Shreveport. Beauty was my black Labrador puppy whom I had welcomed into my life when Ken moved to Hattiesburg.

I enjoyed a high-spirited relief as I saw San Angelo disappearing in my rearview mirror. I was sure I had escaped the shackles of the pirate and that my worst days were behind me.

I was wrong.

Beauty and I wouldn't make it home.

KEELHAULED

Barnacles bejeweled the keel from stem to stern, forming it into the likes of a razor-sharp spinebone of a big fish. Blood would flow from beneath the ship as shells, splinters, and nails would catch and snag the dragging, unstoppable flesh of the keelhauled. The contaminated saltwater stung like the many charged tentacles of a Portuguese man o' war and would often promise the enduring pain of infections and deep scarring. History bears out this savage technique was not intended to end the life of the tortured. Plenty drowned, and many were maimed beyond repair, but most were severely marred and lived out their days as a walking warning to anyone entertaining notions of contesting pirates.

We're on Our Way!

"Don't worry about a thang," Billy droned from beneath his hideout, his Skoal-stained John Deere cap. "I'll ship it all out on Mundy," he promised without even suggesting eye contact as he passed me our spliff for a final toke. "You'll have it in a week or so."

"Thanks for helping me out, man." I sighed in unfamiliar contentment as I exhaled the draw of smoke. "I didn't realize how much stuff I've got."

I couldn't fit all of my possessions into the hatchback of my 1976 Volkswagen Scirocco. So, I left a few boxes for Billy to ship to me in Shreveport.

"Be extra careful with this one." I squinted, emphasizing my concern, as I patted the professionally packaged crate carrying my Pioneer stereo system. "It's gotta make it!"

I was worried about it. It was brand-new, expensive, and, frankly, the only thing I had to show for the job I was leaving.

"This should be more than enough to get it all there." I held out four one-hundred-dollar bills. "You keep the rest, for your trouble."

"Ah, man. Really? You don't have to do that." He grabbed the cash and stuffed it into his grungy pocket. "I'm just glad to help."

We finished our joint in clumsy conversation, just as unsure about each other and equally uncomfortable as the day we'd met.

"For the road," he mumbled as he handed me a six-pack of chilled Miller Beer. "Be safe."

Ironic.

"Come on, girl!" A blast of West Texas cold wind rushed us as I opened the door for Beauty. Just big enough to jump in on her own, she loved riding in the car. I had laid a blanket and her favorite toy on the floorboard for her to be comfortable and warm. She knew it was her spot.

The sunless sky seemed heartless, low and heavy, pressing down with thick clouds of gradient grays, giving the appearance of subzero temperatures. But I felt my spirit rise above the drab when I started my car and the instrumental part of Kansas's "Carry On Wayward Son" was on the radio.

I cranked it up as loud as my speakers allowed, twisted off the cap of a beer, secured my cloak of invincibility, and settled in for the drive.

The warmth of home drawing me eastward flushed my soul as I rolled out of the driveway of the apartment complex for the final time.

Man, am I ready to get out of here. I struggled to believe this was really happening.

"We're on our way!" I announced as much to myself as to Beauty.

Tingles of excitement washed over me as I relished in the sense of departure.

Airborne

After hours of driving, and drinking, the world became dreamlike. The winter gloom didn't improve. It was midafternoon but looked more like an eerily darkening, late-evening sky.

I was well into my second six-pack of beer, just on the east side of Dallas, on Interstate 20, when Beauty began to whine. We both needed to stop.

There were no exit ramps in sight. I turned up the tunes and drove on. Mile after mile, our brimming condition became consequential.

At long last, I saw a sign that read, *Tyler: 20 mi.* It was posted on a narrow, treeless, looping exit eventually pushing us south.

There were no vehicles in either direction. Still, for whatever reason, I fumbled on my blinker and merged to the right to take the off-ramp. Woozily, I awakened to the fact I'd entered the tight loop with far more speed than I or the curve could handle.

Oh no.

I was too boozed to act.

I batted my eyes and shook my head vigorously to clear my field of vision. Making matters considerably worse were clusters of invisible slicks of ice masking the road.

In a frozen frenzy, I overreacted. I hammered the brakes, slipping us into a long, frictionless glide. I had no control over my senses, my limbs, my car, my life.

My reflexes were hopelessly MIA. I'm shamefaced to tell you I watched the unspeakable happen from the numbskull-numb seat of my flying Volkswagen Scirocco.

Thudung! I rammed the embankment harder than you can imagine. It served as a kind of launching ramp.

I'll forever live with the image of sweet Beauty, tongue flapping and all, zipping past my face as the car sailed, perfectly airborne. Later, the sheriff informed me that my little Scirocco had vaulted over two Texas-sized boulders.

Klaashk! The force of the collision with the culvert broke my seat from its rack. My knees smashed into the lower console, wedging a good portion of my body beneath the steering wheel. The top part of my body lashed into a kind of whip motion, shoving my left cheek and ear into the center hub of the steering wheel.

When the car came down and cracked the earth, the earth hit back, with feeling!

The front and rear axles snapped on impact, leaving the car to grind to a halt on top of the four tires.

Phsssssss! Still rocking, I could hear a crushed tire and see radiator steam spewing from the crumpled hood. Like an explosion, both the driver's door and the passenger's had blown open on impact.

I don't know if it was the booze or the bruise, but when I put my left foot down to get out of the car, I went all the way to the ground. Falling, I was able to keep my head from striking a sharp corner of twisted fender.

The smells of scorched rubber and boiling water from an angry engine clashed with the brisk, stone-quiet air. Totally unlearned in all things automobiles, the strange wrecked car smells and sounds caused me great worry. I didn't know if it was going to catch on fire or maybe even blow up.

I staggered away as quickly as I could and plopped down on the ground next to one of the boulders. I braced against the cold, hard, unsympathetic stone for a considerable time, stunned, frozen in serene shock.

"Beauty? Come here, girl!" I was relieved as she bounded from the back of the car, yipping and playful. She hadn't been hurt at all.

Me? I felt like I'd been whacked with a lead pipe across both of my knees and my chest.

Miraculously, all I would suffer from this wreck were banged-up knees, swollen wrists, and a bruised, tender-to-the-touch face for a couple of weeks; no broken bones.

Beauty and I crouched together for a while. I looked at her. She looked at me. The only living beings there for each other at such a harrowing moment and empty place. The ephemeral clouds we created with each breath reminded me to not forget we all have a limited number of them.

"I'm sorry, girl."

I carried her back to her blanket, put on my jacket, and looked for signs of life in every direction. There wasn't so much as a telephone pole rising above the horizon.

Boondocks. Freezing boondocks.

Buried in Kaufman County

I watched the strobing red and blue of the sherriff's car slowly approaching in cold, dead, silence. Haunting.

After a lot of staring and glaring, and a long string of commands given into the mouthpiece of his CB radio, the officer left the engine and lights running, put on his hat, and rambled over to my general area.

With a pinched mouth and crumpled brow, he looked all around, evaluating, deciding. "Hmm." He loaded his jaw with chaw and finally spoke.

"Well, I reckon you're gettin' 'long ahright." The slow-moving, slow-talking deputy, as much questioning as he was evaluating, affirmed I didn't need medical care.

"Yes, sir," I lied, patting my sore face, pulling and squeezing on my arms and joints to convince him and myself. "I'm fine."

"Let's have a look atcher ... driver's license." He tugged and twisted, cinched and snorted a cough, all at the same time, recalibrating his gun belt beneath his jacket.

He tossed his head back to enlist the service of his bifocals. Like the weather, slow and stalled, back and forth, he studied my face and my ID as though he couldn't settle if it and I agreed.

"Lu-zanna, boy, huh?" He spoke with ease, like flowing water over smooth stones. Very comforting.

"Yes, sir," I confirmed. "I should've kept driving 'til I was out of Texas."

He grinned and nodded dubiously as he passed it back to me.

"You by yourself out here, Arthur?"

Before I could answer, he stooped low and ventured his head inside of my jam-packed car.

It's all over now. I was ashamed knowing what he was about to find.

"Hey, little 'un." He brushed Beauty's ears back and took a long look into her curious eyes. "Yer pup, alright?"

"I believe so. She needed a break ... I came off of the ... the highway ... and didn't realize ... I was ..."

"Well," he interrupted, raising his hand for me to stop talking, and skillfully, if not artfully, spitting his tobacco. "Let's hold on for a sec. Let's back up."

He reached into the back floorboard and ponderously pulled out one of the umpteen bottles he'd found. He turned and locked his I've-seen-it-all-before eyes on my I-don't-know-how-that-got-there-officer eyes. Without a flinch or a blink, he slowly poured out the remaining beer onto an ice-covered rock.

"Weren't piddlin' around here, were ya, Arthur?" He raised the bottle up to our eye levels, "You'd been at this for a while, hadn'cha?"

Biting my lower lip, I nodded in nervous admittance, looking to the ground.

"Wontcha step right o're yonder." His brawny hand pointed to a distant spot. He wanted to watch me walk.

With his other hand, he took off his felt-banded Stetson and laid it gently in the center of the hood of his patrol car. The silent rotating pulse of red and blue added even more dread to the gloomy spectacle.

"Let's see what we've got." He shifted his worn-out toothpick to the other side of his mouth as he gently hooked his thumbs behind his hubcap of a belt buckle.

As aimed as I could be, I struggled to land on the mark he had in mind. I stumbled, coming dangerously close to falling to the ground.

"You're all right!" He reached and caught my arm to steady me. "You're all right."

My reactions were dull, and my limbs were unmanageable.

"Look right here, now." He held up his right forefinger in front of his long handlebar mustache. The natural crackle of his leather jacket fostered his relaxed composure. I was encircled with a mixture of Vitalis and Redman.

"Ya gotta good whelp, dintcha ya?" He zoomed in on my cheek, turning his head away just long enough to expectorate and rearrange his chew.

"Looks like ya got punched by the wheel or the mirror, one. Watch close, now." He squinted as he instructed and inspected.

He drew a circle in the air.

I followed his finger with my eyes and nearly fell over.

I'm gonna puke. Overwhelming nausea.

I toppled into a lean on the hood of his Ford Victoria.

"Yes, sir." He sighed. "You've been at this awhile. By the look of these tracks," he surmised, recovering his balding cold head with his warmed hat, "you must have come right o're these rocks here."

116

He locked his gaze onto mine and said, solemnly, "A few feet shy, and they coulda been the death of ya."

I was focused on standing. At the moment, his computations had no impact on me. My brain continued to buffer for hours before his ruling would arrest my attention.

"Oh … kay, Arthur," he called out, finally emerging from his glowing cabin and paperwork. "Let's get you and your pup warm."

He took me by my arm and helped me to my feet.

"You got everything you need from your car?"

"Yes, sir." I nodded. "Thank you."

"I'm not gonna cuff ya, but you and your pup'll have to ride in the back."

He knew I wasn't going to do anything stupid. Still, the backseat of his cruiser was caged.

"It's the law when you're arrested in Kaufman County."

Calmly, he Mirandized me as he opened the back door, unhurriedly motioning for me to get in.

Inside, behind bars, I cradled Beauty with the care I couldn't offer myself.

I sure hadn't seen this as part of my trip home. *Now what?*

"I radioed Big Yella to come and … collect your car. He'll tow 'er in for ya, but she's done, that one." He announced with certainty. "You'll not drive her again."

Sure enough, my car was totaled and buried in Kaufman County, Texas.

You're a Wreck!

"Hey Dad, I'm sorry to bother you," I slurred. "But I'm hoping you can come and get me. I've wrecked my car in Tyler."

I felt the bite of disappointment as my words returned to pierce my ears through the hollow phone.

"Oh, Art!" My dad asked sympathetically with an edge of suspicion, "Are you okay?"

"Yeah. I'm okay."

"What happened?"

"Well, Beauty started whining," I explained, "so I knew she needed a break. I was gettin' off the highway, and I hit a patch of ice. My car slid down a ditch and then up an embankment."

My gut wrenched, torn up by the pain I was bringing to his heart again.

I waited, hoping I'd said enough.

"The car is undrivable. The officer said that both of the axles are broken."

"Are you hurt?" He wondered with a tempered voice. "What about Beauty?"

"We're fine. A little bruised, but fine." I wagged my head and pounded my fist in disgust and disbelief as I levied the weight of my request. "I'm sure sorry, Dad."

"Okay. Thank God you're not hurt. We'll be there soon."

Lying to my parents, and everyone else for that matter, came all too easy for me. I had convinced myself it was nothing personal. This was just the way the pirate and I needed to govern my life. The Father of Lies had persuaded me this is how everyone gets along in the world. Deceiving, stealing, manipulating, and many other vices; these were the colors now flying over my ship.

I never told my parents I'd been drinking or had been arrested. I felt like the truth would be more than their tender hearts could handle. I lied, more so, hoping they'd think more highly of me than what I'd become. I had lost all respect for myself and was sure that no one else placed any honor on my life, either.

I was arrested for driving while intoxicated in Kaufman County, Texas, where they have a no-tolerance policy. This meant I could either be held in jail until I stood before the judge to receive my sentence, or I could pay the bail, go home, and return at a later date for my day in court.

I had three hundred dollars on me, the exact amount needed to cover the bail.

Drained, I slouched at the cashier's window, waiting for someone to take my money. As I pulled out the wad of cash, a buried baggie of pot, and two Quaaludes, fell out of my pocket and onto the floor.

Oh, my God!

Like lightning, I crouched to tie my shoe, grabbed the dope, and slipped it into my coat pocket. I picked up Beauty to maximize distraction.

Breathe.

It would've been a different story had the deputies searched me or required me to empty my pockets. I was carrying a large amount of cannabis, an eight ball of cocaine, and five tabs of speed wrapped in foil. They never checked.

The heater in my parents' car diffused a comforting, homey fume that reached my heart as quickly as it had my nose. The roar of the fan on high delayed the inevitable and somewhat insulated the tension we were all suffering. Relieved to have finally made it up to the main freeway, my dad flipped the heater off and spoke.

"From the hospital to the jailhouse." He struggled to find me in the rearview mirror because I had intentionally sat directly behind him. "You look a wreck. What's going on, Art?"

I had no plan, no intention, and no words to reply.

My mom was disturbed by my lack of response. She turned all the way around in her front seat, rose to her knees until her shoulders were squared and she could look straight at me.

Fixed stiff and staring at her in wonder, I watched her tiny hand reach for the dome light. I looked away the second it came on.

Oh, please, don't look at me.

Heart pounding, my chest tightened and my breath shallowed to all but a heave.

Who knows what she could discern? Mothers are like that.

She leaned over the back of her seat. I broke into a sweat. She leaned her face close to mine, deliberately sniffing the air as though she smelled something. She didn't say anything, she only cupped her hand under her chin and thoughtfully tapped her lips with her cameo-ringed forefinger.

In the dim light, she tilted and dipped her head in every possible angle to evaluate my cuts and bruises. With intense concern and not remotely satisfied, she twisted up her mouth and turned around to sit in her seat. As she did, she locked and held her eyes on mine until she couldn't.

How much does she know?

What did she see?

"This could have been so much worse," she whispered. "What's happening with you?" she pleaded through frustrating bewilderment.

Drained from the drama and drink, it felt good to lean my head against the cold window. I peered through my secret reflection, the one only you can see when your face is leaning on the glass, out into the darkness of the desert.

"I don't know," I mumbled. "I'm wondering that myself."

Once the Raider handily hoisted his flag over my life, his true colors began to really fly. He threw me, broken and bound, overboard. Weighted with addictions and fears, burdened with sorrows and regrets. Bumping along the sharp belly of the ship, I was slashed and gashed and lost a lot of blood, most, if not all, of my dreams, and life by the gallon. Every direction I looked, my life had been razed to the ground.

Like a frantic forensic, I spent the torturous two-hour drive to Shreveport examining the tragic scenes of my life. I unearthed every front and field, sieved through mounds of memories searching for something that would make me feel happier, hopeful.

Nothing.

My existence had devolved to one of desperate survival.

Then, as we were driving under the lights of my neighborhood, an idea, buried deep beneath loads of debris and disappointments, flashed like a small fleck of gold. When it gleamed, by God's grace, I caught a breath of air.

Maybe.

Maybe she would still remember me.

Breath of Hope

I've known Wendy for forty years and still recall, with heart-racing detail, the first time I saw her. Her elegance and kindness, and her cheerful blue eyes that shined at a distance broke through my aches and pains and a 103-degree fever. I had the flu.

Wendy was the hostess of a Mexican restaurant my brother had discovered on the main drag, not long after we had moved to Shreveport. My family had met there for dinner, but I ended up having to leave without eating because I was feeling so yucky.

As murky as my mind was, this sweet-tea, southern-drawled beauty had been made an impact on my young heart.

So much was the impression Wendy had on me that, months later, when she walked into the small dime store where I worked, I recognized her as the girl of my dreams who had served me chips and salsa.

When the grapevine delivered the news that she'd been hired as a clerk, in the same store where I was a stockman, I was hurled into excitement and dread at the prospect of seeing her every day.

What if I have to talk to her?

You're an idiot. What chance do you have of ever talking to her?

What if she finds out I'm a dopehead?

Someone like her would never have anything to do with someone like me.

I didn't venture too close right away and for a good reason. Every one of my friends had asked her out, and she had told every one of them no. I'd already experienced a significant amount of rejection in my life and wasn't interested in standing in line for more.

Later, she revealed that she'd been waiting for me to ask. I couldn't have even imagined it.

"She's beautiful," Ken affirmed. "Too pretty for you, that's for sure!"

"Don't I know it." I puffed my cheeks to embellish a forceful sigh.

"Don't even try, dude," Ken sagaciously advised. "Don't even try."

I didn't have the confidence or the words to speak to the most beautiful lady I'd ever seen in my life, much less, and I do mean *much* less, the confidence to ask her out on a date! I didn't even try for the longest time.

After seeing Wendy at work, almost daily, for a good long while, I finally approached her. With my head bowed, I apprehensively suggested to her that maybe … she probably wouldn't want to, but in the case that she might … she'd want to go on a date …with me.

She said yes! That she'd love to! I was floored! My brother couldn't believe it any more than I could. I was elated!

But there was a fly in the resplendent ointment: On the night of our date, sitting on the swing behind her mama's house, under shimmering stars, I told her of my new job and that I'd be leaving for San Angelo the next morning.

We were both terribly disheartened. But my word had been given, and I felt bound to go. Had I known then what I know now, I would have never left her. Of course, that's not how our lives are navigated, especially when you're eighteen years old. I had the hollow feeling I was sailing away from the warm, safe lights of home.

I wouldn't see Wendy again for months. She wrote to me often while I was in San Angelo. Amid my West Texas world of chaos, crowds, and critics, her words watered my tired and searching soul.

I came to count on Wendy's letters. Like her ship, her words were full of life and truth; they carried purpose. Sometimes she'd include a Bible verse or a poem she'd created.

In one of her notes, she penned a prayer to God for me. It needled my heart in some tender way. I hid that one deep into my canvas duffle bag I kept at my bedside table and would read it again and again.

Like throwing a mooring rope to a passing ship, words, sent by Wendy's hand and God's heart, worked hard to catch my wandering heart and scattered mind.

In response to her many loving and encouraging letters, I wrote her back, once, or maybe twice, at the most. In immaturity and youthful zeal, in selfishness, frankly, I was sailing detached from things and people I thought would weigh me down.

The older I grow, the more I understand that God uses people and opportunities not so much to weigh us down but to help anchor us. I couldn't see it at the time.

The Call

We made it to my parent's house at one o'clock in the morning. While I fixed a place in the garage for Beauty to sleep, I allowed my mind to wonder, only so slightly, toward the chance that Wendy might still be a friend. By now, I was certain, she'd been found by a gentleman and would have moved on with her life.

I'll just call to let her know that her letters meant a lot to me.
That's all.
I'll just call her.

I dithered for days. Not only was I unsettled and nervous, but I was reeling from being arrested, totaling my car, and, after nine months of living away and unbridled, having to move back into my parents' house. As well, I was keenly aware that I had likely hurt Wendy's feelings by not writing to her while I was in Texas. I wondered if she would even want to talk to me.

On a Saturday morning, when I was the only one home, unexpected bravery rose in my heart. Quickly, to the phone. I slowly dialed Wendy's number.

"Hello?" The kind answer calmed me a little.

"Hello? Mrs. Wasson?" I asked, nauseated and dizzy. There was no turning back now.

"Yes. Who's this?"

"This is Art. Art Evans. Is …Wendy available to talk?"

"Well, let me see." After the clacking of the handset coming to rest on the table, I could hear her lifted voice, "Wendy? Wendy? Telephone."

"Hello?" My heart leaped out of my chest, and my breath abandoned me when I heard Wendy's strong and familiar voice. I wasn't prepared for the moment.

"Hello?" she asked for a second time as I searched for my winged words.

"Hey. Hi, Wendy."

Breathe.

"It's Art."

"Art! Hi! How are you?" Wendy asked with a sincerity that, outside of my family, I hadn't encountered in a long time. Just as sweet as I had remembered. "I wasn't sure if I'd ever hear from you again."

"Well, I … I'm sorry about that. But I'm here … I'm in Shreveport now. I've moved back."

So far, so good.

"I just want to tell you that I'm really thankful for your letters. I … saved some of 'em."

Oh, my gosh! You sound so positively creepy! The pirate never missed his opportunity to mock. *She'll have nothing to do with you now, for sure!*

"It really means a lot that you would write to me," I gushed.

"You're welcome! I hope I didn't write too much." She laughed softly.

"No! No, you didn't," I assured her. "I'm sure sorry that I didn't write you back very much. I'm not really the writin' kind, ya know?"

"Oh, that's okay. Don't worry about that at all. I'm glad you're back!"

Unlike the many broken and bruised people I had encountered over the previous months, her voice was clear and bright. It was coming from a whole person. We talked for a few minutes.

"Would you like to get some pizza?" I asked before I realized what I had done. Wendy seemed as surprised as I was.

I held my breath.

"That would be great! What time should I be ready?"

I was over the moon to discover that though Wendy had lots of friends, she didn't have a boyfriend. Still, I couldn't fathom she'd be willing to seriously date me.

"You sure seem excited when you talk about her," my dad commented, through sips of coffee and his gentle smile.

"Well, I sure like her, Dad," I answered shyly. "Wendy's one of the nicest people I know. And she's beautiful!"

"Yep, she is," he agreed. "There's something very special about her."

Somebody Coulda Died!

"Arthur Evans. Is that your name, son?" The judge asked sternly from his lofty bench. He shuffled through a stack of papers my appointed counsel had just handed to him.

"Yes, sir," I replied, squinting to appear as sincere, and sober, as possible.

"Let me ask you something." He looked up and leaned toward me, resting on his robed elbows. He dipped his chin to see over his glasses.

"What if you'd hit somebody with your car out there?" he asked flatly. "I reckon you'd be tellin' a different story by now, don't you?"

His gravelly voice echoed around the concrete walls of the small, bare room the color of diluted Pepto Bismol.

"Yes, sir." I wagged my head slowly. "That would have been horrible. I'm sorry—"

"Ya realize you coulda killed somebody?" Like the arrow of a skilled archer, his rebuke hit its mark. "'Bout near killed yourself, dincha?!"

I was speechless as I weighed his words and what could have been.

"Huh? Do you hear me?" He clutched the high arms of his old high-back leather chair. "Somebody coulda died ... right out there on Interstate 20! Coulda died! ... because of your blasted foolishness!"

"Yes, sir." I cringed, inside and out. "I'm sorry."

"Are ya sorry for whatcha done? Or ya sorry for gettin' caught?!"

"Well, I'm—"

"Don't answer!" He held up his hand like he was stopping traffic. "I know the answer to my own question." His voice faded as he stared down and resumed his interest in shuffling.

He didn't look up when he stoically informed me, "I could putcha in jail, ya know?" Long pause. "Take yer driver's license from ya ... hold you here for a while." Longer pause.

"But ... since this is your first arrest, and last, I hope"—his eyes lifted to the ceiling as he followed his thoughts—"here's what we're gonna do. I'm fining you a thousand dollars to be paid within ninety days. It could be twice that, ya know?" He interrupted himself.

"And you're gonna check in with our probation office on the twenty-first of the month, for the next twenty-four months." He peered down at me from his bench.

"Yes, sir. I ..."

"Don't ...be ...late!"

"And, Mr. Evans," he waited until he was sure he held my complete attention, "don't ever ... let me see you in my courtroom again!"

I made the drive from Shreveport to Kaufman County every month, two hours both ways. When I'd arrive at the probation office, the officer I'd been assigned to wasn't necessarily available on the spot. I'd always have to wait at least thirty minutes, sometimes as long as an hour and a half. The meeting itself was usually wrapped up in fifteen minutes or so. The five-to-six-hour turnaround trip wasn't my real problem.

I didn't have a car or a job. What I did have was a thousand-dollar fine that had to be paid in three months, and an addiction to alcohol, speed, and weed.

What am I going to do?

I know what I should have done.

The pirate's colors flying over my ship couldn't make me utterly unconscious to the yanking of my heart. But as you understand, knowing the best direction and actually taking it are two different things. So, the pirate and I ratcheted up my well-tuned, proven-to-get-me-through tactic: I lied.

I lied to my parents about why I needed to borrow their car, strangely, on the twenty-first of each month. Replaying some of the desperate appeals I made to my dad to use his car, I'm embarrassed. In that do-or-die pressure cooker, I wasn't thinking very smartly. I came up with some real doozies he likely saw right through.

I had to pay the fine, refill the gas tank, and, as a nineteen-year-old young man, do life. I needed money, and lots of it. So, I stole from my mother's purse and my dad's wallet. I resumed old and dangerous relationships to generate cash by selling drugs.

Like the puppet all tied up and tangled, here I was again, bound hand and foot to the pleasure and profit of the pirate.

This One Is Mine

When the pirate gains such control that he's able to successfully raise his flag over your ship, he's declaring to all others: *This one is now mine! Refit and renamed, he'll now serve at my pleasure and for my purposes.*

The Jolly Roger (the general term for a pirate's flag) appears in many forms. The pennants brandished on the mast of my ship would alternate, broadcasting the presence of different pirates and their diabolical influences: pride, addictions, rage, fears, deception, rejection, loneliness—and the list goes on.

This is imperative to understand: I wasn't sampling pot or cocaine, I was a hooked peddler. I wasn't socially drinking on the weekends. Bibulous, I drank every day to the point it was difficult for me to go to sleep without the numbness booze brings. Nor did I fib now and then; I was a live-or-die-by-the-lie person. These vices had become "the ropes" of my pirate-conquered vessel.

I wasn't kind, considerate, or thoughtful. I was sullen, mean, and conducted myself with pronounced selfishness. I wasn't able to help others because I couldn't help myself.

I had become a contributing crony, a collaborator with the pirate's armada. I'd been marked by his colors now covering and governing my life, my relationships, my destiny. I did all I could to hide all I could from my folks and Wendy. I shuddered at the idea of them finding out who and what I really was.

It all seemed to be smooth sailin'.

Until.

Until I had a face-to-face encounter with the savage of my soul. It sounds strange to say it, but the Devil went too far. As you will see.

FACE-TO-FACE

Throughout the Golden Age of Piracy, 1650–1720, the cutthroats held unimaginable power over the seven seas. They ruled by fathomless fear. Not only were they homicidal henchmen, but pirates also struck massive terror into the hearts of sailors by elevating their skills of torture to ineffable perfection.

Floggings, keelhaulings, and tying captives to the high mast for great lengths of time were common punishments for those refusing to cooperate. Many of the disobedient were blinded. Not by gouging but by a rope squeezed around their foreheads until their eyeballs ejected from their sockets.

In some cases, rather than quickly ending the life of their prey, the savages would cut them into pieces, slow enough for the sufferer, all the while bleeding out, to watch his severed body parts be devoured by hungry sharks.

"I can't help you, Art!" Wendy poured out of her heart. "I just want God's best for you."

We'd been dating for a couple of months when she unmasked enough about my ways and ruinous wonts to draw a line in the sand.

"I'm in no position to tell you what to do with your life. But I'm going to follow Jesus. If you're going to have anything to do with me, you'll have to put down your drugs and your booze and follow Jesus, too."

Oh, how badly I wanted to. I like to believe I would have surrendered all, had I realized Jesus was waiting and able to route the enemy and take command of my ship. But at the moment, I just couldn't imagine it happening.

Pirates were running around on every deck of my vessel, barking out orders and threats to my life, my secrets, and habits. So, as cowardly as before, I took the low road. To the delight of the deceiver, I revealed my true colors. I lied.

"Okay, I will," I promised flimsily. "I'll stop."

"I love God, you know?" I was trying to convince myself as much as I was her. "I'll get this right."

With pureness of heart, Wendy believed me.

I straight-faced deceived her for months. I thought I could effectively navigate both worlds without harming anyone. I believed I could tame the tiger, you understand. But anytime you yield any part of your life to the pirate, you can count on this: he'll exploit your bargain to the full extent of ruin.

I gave him more than enough leverage to do measurable damage.

Do you remember the children's limerick, *There Was a Young Lady of Niger?*:

> *There was a young lady of Niger*
> *Who smiled as she rode on a tiger;*
> *They returned from the ride*
> *With the lady inside,*
> *And the smile on the face of the tiger.*[4]

When a bully tastes blood, the subjugation of his victim, he can't restrain himself. The hemorrhage triggers an irresistible lust for more— more power and control. The weaknesses he tracks down in others makes an irresistible demand on his native impulses to dominate and destroy all he puts his hands to.

When I thought I had experienced the worst he could dish out, my oppressor snapped his jaw back with a satanic smirk. *You fool! You haven't seen anything yet.*

One fateful Friday night, July 29, 1983, the pirate went too far.

To the Pit!

"Not interested, man," I said, straining to reveal sincerity but not fear.

"Dude, you gotta do this!" Kyle pleaded. "It'll be like ol' times, man! Please?!"

Kyle was a friend, or, I should say, a fellow druggie, who had badgered me into going to an Iron Maiden concert at Hirsch Memorial Coliseum, in Shreveport. I had told Wendy and my parents I was going to a friend's birthday party.

I wasn't excited about being there. It was the "ol' times" that concerned me. About a year and a half earlier, in March of 1982, Ken and I, and a boatload of piratical friends, had gone to an Ozzy Osbourne concert at the same venue.

It wasn't great. As a matter of fact, it had been perfectly tormenting to my soul. Even though at the time I had no fellowship with God, there was a part of me that craved His peace.

If you've never been to a heavy metal concert, it's hard to visualize the density of darkness at such a gathering. This is no evening With Neil Diamond with everyone waving their lighters, singing in unison with Karen Carpenter's "We've Only Just Begun."

If you were to combine rush-hour subway traffic—everyone's tired, ticked, and trying to get home—with driving rock music at the loudest ear-splitting decibel possible, with a generous serving of drugs and drink, you might find yourself on the fringes of a metal concert.

At the Ozzy concert, I was contently perched at the highest row available at the top of the coliseum. I could see the band and the people and, at least partially, regulate the tidal wave of sound pouring from the stacks and stacks of amplifiers on the stage.

I could only tolerate so much of the haunting and propulsive tunes like "Crazy Train," "Children of the Grave," and "Paranoid."

"Let's go, man!" Ken wildly waved his hands for me to follow him.

"Where to?" I asked as I stood up. "Where're we goin'?"

"To the pit!" he exclaimed over his shoulder as he bounded down the concrete steps. "Kyle and Matt are waitin' on us!"

The mosh pit at a rock or punk concert is toward the stage, and it's where individuals gather to intentionally *mosh*, that is, to "dance in a violent manner, jumping, twirling, and deliberately colliding with other dancers."

It's just as ludicrous as it sounds. Not everyone goes into a mosh pit to intentionally hurt others or get hurt. But you most certainly intend to slam others and to be slammed. It's a brush with violence, for sure, if not, for some, a full-bodied encounter.

It wasn't my thing, but Ken was excited for me to go along, and I'd never slam-danced before. I warily consented but kept my guard intense and intact.

Squinting through the darkness, the haze of cigarette and dope smoke, and the billows of fog creeping from the stage, I watched as, a long way off, Kyle and Matt jumped right out into the middle of dozens of moshers. They were swiftly swept away and devoured like ragdolls in a hurricane. I winced.

Reluctantly, I stepped into the closest edge of the pit and was promptly nailed in the face by a spinning girl's sequined elbow.

Perfect. Now I have a reason to go back to my safe seat!

My enthusiastic and unrelenting brother wasn't about to let that happen.

"Come on!" Ken grabbed me by my arm and dragged me into the craziness. Instinctively, I ducked my head and plowed through until the pulling stopped.

Somewhere out in the middle of the tumultuous tide, I raised my head. At that moment, if it's possible, the music got louder, the screams more piercing, and the violence more ferocious. I had been dragged to the pith of the pit.

Both menfolk and womenfolk were throwing punches at one another! Remarkably, as one sixty-plus Ozzy look-alike was struck, he laughed as though someone had just hit him with a surprise punchline rather than a punch to his face. He was notably numbed by a substance and likely couldn't feel the blow.

This minacious memory took center stage as I was on my way to the Iron Maiden concert. I would certainly not be going near the pit.

Face-to-Face

"Elvis has left the building!" was first uttered at Hirsch Memorial Coliseum in 1957. With seating for only ten thousand, it's a smallish venue. When we washed up for the Iron Maiden concert, it was bursting at the seams.

Not only were there thousands of ticket holders for what must have been a sold-out show, but there was also a gauntlet of hundreds more, pleading with anyone and everyone to sell them their ticket for a profit. I was enthusiastic about the possibility of selling mine.

Had Kyle not intervened, I would have pocketed a hundred dollars and escaped having to enter the nerve center of the macabre, already oozing its sights and sounds to the parking lot.

I was shaken up by the haunted-house melodramatics in every direction. As you already know, I'm a total lightweight when it comes to being scared or spooked. I don't like it and would do all I could to avoid it.

Equally upsetting was seeing a uniformed policeman taking a hit from a joint being passed around in a circle of metalheads. This disturbing incident slapped an ear-ringing welp to my naivety and wedged a splinter of skepticism into my soul that would fester for years.

I was sandwiched between Kyle and Matt as we weaved our way through the mazed masses of skeletons, bearded giants, and many who were donning freakish masks. It was an all-out "Let your freak flag fly!" kind of event. There were enough groupies in costumes to give the overall feel of a derailed Halloween party.

"Let's forget about the seats, man!" Matt screamed over the brawling and crawling commotion. "Let's get to the stage!"

Just as we made it to the massive wall of the eight-foot-high stage, all of the lights in the entire coliseum went out. It was a can't-see-your-hand-in-front-of-your-face dark.

In shared excitement, mixed with palpable fear, there erupted a massive harrowing, ground-shaking scream!

Was it a power outage? A prank? Was it part of the show?

Nobody knew.

I bristled and braced myself, closing my eyes to feel in control of the darkness.

I'm going to lower the third by half a step and write the next few paragraphs in a minor key. For those of you not musically inclined, all that means is, cue the background music of a horror film.

Like the rumblings of a far-off train, we could hear and feel something, someone, approaching. Hissings, hummings, and haunting whispers coming from all directions, layers of sound growing by the second in complexity and volume.

Pitch-black, thick, tangible darkness.

There were gusts of wind that felt like someone had turned on a jumbo oscillating drum fan.

I defensively piqued my ears for cues that might save my life. I could hear distinct expressions of undeniable panic: genuine groans, gasps, and screams.

"W-w-what is that?!" someone spluttered.

"Is that real?" I could feel the concerted recoil of the crowd.

"Far out, man! Is it alive?"

"Is it moving?"

I turned my head to the left and to the right, straining to locate whatever it was others were seeing. I couldn't find a wedge of light except for the tiny dots of the glowing-red EXIT signs at the far edges of the arena.

Suddenly, there was a mind-mauling explosion, melt-your-face loud with a wave of heat I couldn't imagine being any hotter!

In one drilling, piercing punch—lights, smoke, guitars, drums, bizarre sounds at about 150 decibels—and from some unknown source or location, the most fathomless moan you can imagine.

Like accidentally taking hold of a live wire, a full dose of adrenaline and dread diffused into my whole being.

What is that?!

Where is that?!

With my back against the stage wall, figuratively and literally, the band was above and behind me. Bone-rattling music and coldish fog were pouring down and over me.

I was facing the crowd, so, through the dark mist, as an obscure observer, I could see faces and reactions to whatever was happening on the raised platform.

A girl, who I'm sure was older but appeared to be about twelve, was clenching her hair with her fists on both sides of her head, screaming so loudly it seemed like her jaws would dislocate. Several had both hands plastered over their eyes, while others, with eyes wide, shrieked with hysteria.

Unsolicited and without warning, like a heat-seeking missile finds its target, the Spirit of Truth broke through my exposed heart. With a shaft of reality, He opened my eyes and let me see things differently for a frame or two, truthfully, transparently.

I'm doubtless when I say this divine pivot was an answer to the prayers of people who loved me. I'm eternally thankful. Never underestimate the power of God released through faith-filled prayers.

Of all I was taking in, what I was most conscious of was the oneness, the blatant, unified menticide. Jumping and swaying, raising hands and voices, this flock of thousands had been altogether captured and carried away, as if in a trance. Then, the spell was elevated.

"Maiden's tech team was able to create complex robots that literally seem larger than life, such as the Final Frontier-era Eddie, who is muscle bound and nears 10 feet tall," describes rock and metal music magazine *Loudwire.*

Eddie is Iron Maiden's mascot. He's a zombie-like skeletal monster that Maiden refashions to correlate with their current tour. He's been depicted as a cyborg, an Egyptian mummy, a demonized puppeteer controlling a marionette who is the antichrist, and many other personas. He appears on the covers of all the band's albums and is the face of the group. Live and in concerts, Eddie could rise as tall as thirty feet above the band.

With the stage above and behind me, I saw the people's upturned, crazed faces before I saw what they were seeing. Gaping and gasping mouths, eyes stretched and unblinking, screams of terror and fright. Some were shaking their heads so fast and so hard, I thought they would convulse their brains right onto the floor. The real me cared too much to ignore it. This scene would haunt me as much as what came next.

For this show, Maiden's World Piece Tour, Eddie appeared as a ten-foot-tall, lobotomized mental patient. Though his skull had been cut open like the top of a cantaloupe and refastened with a couple of cabinet brackets, he still had waist-long, sheer, and flowing gray hair sprouting from his scabby head. A walking-and-stalking robot with sharply pointed joints and fingers poking their way through lengths of chains and an ultra-grunge straitjacket, his face and movements were sinister as he exhaled red smoke from his mouth and flashed red lights from deep inside his sunken eyes.

Another factor brewing in this perfect storm was that on our way to the concert, we had smoked two joints of marijuana, one of which was saturated with hash oil. Like the hallucinogenic fear toxin used by the Scarecrow, one of Batman's archnemeses, the drugs I had ingested induced a psychoactive state, modifying and magnifying all I was afraid of. By the time of my face-to-face with Eddie, the fear toxins I'd consumed had seized full ownership of my senses. They consumed me.

I whirled to see the spectacle that was so grimly rattling the rabble. The instant I turned, the ten-large ogre was hunching directly over me in a jumped-out-from-behind-the-gravestone-to-shred-your-flesh kinda way.

Groosh! Pushing aside a wall of fog, all herky-jerky, he abruptly trundled toward me. As he moved, he moaned. It may have been the music or well-timed sound effects, I'm not sure. What I am sure of, though, is it was too much for me!

Panicked, I frantically searched in the bedlam for Matt and Kyle. They were nowhere to be found. I was alone and knew it; I felt it.

When I saw Eddie's maggot-munched face, up close, his mouth looked like it belonged to some kind of terrifying sea creatures; rows of yellowed, broken teeth were permanently fixed in a snarl! It seemed like Eddie was alive, and he was controlling everything and everybody. Of course, all of this was fake; my fear wasn't.

When I turned to run, I was blocked, not in an innocent-crowd way, but in a tauntingly cruel way. The rampart of rockers who resisted me thought either I was fooling around and they were going to play along or that they were fulfilling some kind of civil code, propping up a fellow human in requiring me to face my fears. Either way, there was no way they were even *about* to keep me there!

"Let me through!" I shouted, triggering even more raw reflexes from the edge-of-riot crowd. Three or four put their hands on my shoulders and head and pushed me back to the stage.

"Let me out! Please!" Nobody budged.

"Hargh! Ha! Ha!" Plenty jeered, while others, pointing, cheered them on.

"Get back up there, you chicken!" (I'm sparing you the free-flowing vulgarities.) A hulking man, wearing a carved pumpkin-head mask, with a ghastly guffaw, pulled me toward Eddie with yank-your-shoulder-out-of-socket intensity. I thought he was going to hoist me up and toss me onto the stage.

I was overtaken by fear.

"Please!" I pleaded. "I'm not kidding! Let me go!"

Suddenly, like Moses parting the Red Sea, the pumpkin-head man raised his hands and his voice in my favor.

"Move! Get out of the way!" He thundered the command. "This man's gotta get through!"

The dense mob parted just enough for me to force my escape. Bumping and banging into people, brain-shocked as I bounced from ear-splitting scream to the next, I bungled my way toward the exit as quickly as I could.

I'll never forget the look on the face of the security guard, posted at my getaway door. His eloquent expression said, *Uh-huh. What are you doing here, anyway? You know you don't belong here.*

He was right.

Art had left the building!

I had run a mile or so, into another part of town, before I turned around to confirm no one was after me. Silly, I know. At the time, brain-in-a-blender panic!

Breakdown to Breakthrough

As only Jehovah Shalom (God of Peace) can do, He took what the pirate of fear had designed for my disgrace and destruction and turned it to my benefit and favor.

What I couldn't discern in the commotion of the moment God soon allowed me to fully understand. Here's what I mean. When I faced Eddie, Iron Maiden's monstrous mascot, God allowed me to recognize, with my natural eyes, what the eyes of my heart had been fighting to reveal to me for some time, what I had steadfastly refused to see.

136

The Spirit of Truth had let me come eye to eye with the spirit of death and destruction, the pirate who had been driving my ship for years. I wasn't running away from Eddie any more than he was the author of my horror. I had wrestled my way through the horde and run to the point of breathlessness to get away from the spirit of fear himself.

You can see my dilemma: I couldn't outrun him whom I'd invited, at least welcomed, to board and steer my ship. In quenchless greed, he had yanked and torn, hounded and harried, undermined and overwhelmed every part of my life. I was wedge-driven to the absolute end of myself. With no escape, nowhere else to run, everything in me came to a grinding halt.

I had run straight into what the Psalmist David calls "the pit." It was deep, dark, and immensely dangerous. It felt like my grave.

But God ...

Here I was, in the overmastering clutches of epic King James version fear, the unrelenting squeeze of shame choking out the slightest sliver of light and hope. At the most unbearable moment, when it seemed my life could not become any worse, Jesus threw back the curtain and enabled me to see what was truly happening.

I was breaking down, but God's love was breaking through. He, the only real Grave Robber, would soon break me out!

God can do in an instant what we couldn't accomplish in a lifetime. He can flip the tables of your enemy's entire battle plans with a single Word.

We're often waiting for one whom we care about, who's in trouble, to wise up, which can certainly happen. But for many, like me, the life-changing breakthrough isn't the result of your friend suddenly getting smart or instantaneously arriving at maturity. Usually, it's a work of God's steady and merciful hand doing what only He can do. More often than not, He unlocks hearts in response to our prayers.

Never give up on anyone's eyes being opened. All the while the pirate is maligning and maneuvering, the Prince of Life is watching and working to save, deliver, heal, and restore.

This small crack in my stony heart would quickly lead to the breaking of many strongholds that were governing my mind and will. I'm forever thankful.

I had given so much of my life, my energies and efforts, time and talents, affections and attitudes to the promise-giving, promise-breaking pirate. I was being held hostage by deceptive and demented forces far more powerful than me. God assured me if I would trust Him and follow His lead, He'd heal my heart, my mind, my life. He gave me His Word, He would make me free.

I hadn't prayed for a long time. As I sat alone at the kitchen table in my parents' house, physically and emotionally shaking from my meet-and-greet with terror, with my head in my hands, I timidly whispered heavenward.

"I'm sorry for ruining my life, God. I know You love me and have a plan for my life. Please help me! Will You forgive me for all of my sins and wash me clean? I don't know how You can ever forgive me for what I've done? I give You my heart, God. I want You to be my Father. Please help me! Please help me."

Before I finished breathing this simple prayer of repentance, Jesus's gracious Spirit had found me, surrounded me, and had raised His sword over me like a soldier protecting his fallen brother on the battlefield.

Like the warrior, David declared, "I put all my hope in the Lord. He leaned down to me; He listened to my cry for help. He lifted me out of the pit of death, out of the mud and filth, and set my feet on solid rock. He steadied my legs." (Psalm 40:1-2)

I am privileged to have known His powerful presence from that moment until now. Even as I'm writing of His unwavering love toward us all, I am humbled, awed, and thankful that He would save me.

Just as quickly, like walking into a dark house and going from room to room, flipping on all the lights, Jesus's Spirit of Truth flooded every space of my soul. Rooms were swollen with sins and festering with shame. Hallways, like clogged arteries, were choked by anxieties, anger, and affliction. Closets were stuffed deep and high with despair and disappointments.

My life was filthy and infested with pride and arrogance, hiding and hoarding all my failures and fears, and many other rotting things the pirate and I had haphazardly dumped into my heart. Walking into a moldering milieu, as it were, where something had died but had not been buried, my soul diffused the rancid stench of death and decay.

With the clarity and care of an Emergency Room doctor who knows time is running out for his patient, Jesus entreated, "We have to take care of all of this."

"Yes, I know."

As the sickly patient who, for the longest time, resisted seeing the doctor because of embarrassment, and was doubly embarrassed because of his worsened condition, I yielded the best I knew how. His tender kindness and understanding startled me.

Cloaks and Guises

Jesus brought me to the innermost chamber of my heart. He gently pushed open the shadowy door and stood to the side as He pointed inside to the exceptionally well-ordered room.

"If you'll give Me this one, Art, the cleaning and the healing of the rest of your house will go much easier."

I felt deeply saddened and ashamed. I had convinced myself that no one but me knew about this room. I mean nobody, not even God. But alas, here we were.

I slunk past Him and stood, hunched, in the middle of the room. Slowly, soberly, I turned to survey the items filling the scads of shelves, all different lengths and heights, lining the walls.

I recognized the host of masks I'd invented over the years. Some were old, which I hadn't seen or even thought of in a long time. Others were awfully familiar as I systematically, habitually interchanged them.

I knew what He was asking of me. He wasn't listening for an answer, He was looking for one. I was clear about what I had to do.

Heart-to- Heart

"Can we talk?" I mumbled somberly.

"Sure," Wendy replied cheerfully. "What's up?"

"No, I mean, can you come here, to my house? I need to talk to you."

"Oh, okay. That's fine." Wendy sensed my failing spirit. "I can be there in an hour or so."

"Okay, see you then."

The second I hung up the phone, the threatened pirate lambasted my soul with anxiety and pending rejection.

You're really going to do this?
You shouldn't tell her a thing.
You're an idiot! Don't do it.
She'll never trust you again.

Still harnessed with my habits, I went straight to my mask room. Or, I should say, my false identity room. I scanned the shelves, trying to decide which story, which persona, would be the best approach. God's strong but gracious Spirit interrupted me.

"There's no help for you in here, Art."

He smiled gently with his confrontation, at once comforting me with His compassion and covering me with dignity.

"Let Me help you. We can do this together. Give me this room, and I'll make you free."

"How was the birthday party?" Wendy asked nervously.

Caringly, she sat down next to me on the couch in the warm, dimly lit den of my parents' house. She bolstered her guard by arranging one of the throw pillows across her lap. I could see in her beautiful, starkly clear cobalt eyes, looking trustingly into mine, she deemed whatever this was about as serious. She leaned in, eager for me to speak.

I took a deep breath and ignored her question and the notion of smiling.

"I need to tell you something." I struggled to endure looking into her eyes. "It's ...very important ... and ... difficult."

"Okay," she said with sheltered confidence. "Whatever it is, I'm sure it's going to be fine."

She covered my cold and wringing hands with her own as she smiled. "Don't worry."

"I'm sorry, Wendy." I closed my eyes to focus and steady my breath. "But I'm not who you think I am."

I opened my eyes to confirm I'd actually said the words out loud.

She drew a deep breath as her eyebrows raised with intrigue and concern. Her smile only barely faded as she slowly withdrew her comforting hands.

"You're so kind and honest," I continued. "And I love that about you."

I was instinctively contriving to sidestep the issue if not save my skin. Forcefully, abruptly, desperately, the real me rose up.

"I'm selfish. I'm addicted to drugs, and I drink too much!"

Taking advantage of the gushing underground fountain which had finally found its way through, I spit out as much of the truth, all at once, as possible.

"I've been lying to you for months!"

"What do you mean?" She asked in earnest but calculated calm.

"I told you that I would stop smoking pot, stop using drugs, and that I wouldn't drink anymore." I bowed my wagging head. "I haven't stopped any of it! I've just been lying and lying and lying to you, Wendy. I'm sorry. I'm so sorry."

Watching furrows of empathy form around her eyes as they slowly filled with tears, broke my heart. I felt her heart of compassion and mercy. I began to weep.

Now, I'm not saying that crying is all that! I mean, I had cried in pain, in regrets, and such. But I'd not cried tears of genuine remorse for a lot of years. The floodgates broke open as my weeping turned into a long, irrepressible sob, with heaves and the works. Wendy took hold of my hands and held on as though I was going over Niagara.

When I gathered enough composure to speak, I let her know I had no expectations of our future. "I understand if you never want to talk to me again, Wendy."

"What?" she said as her eyes lit with renewed fire. "Why would you say that? I forgive you, Art. God is bigger than all of this!"

I felt like I'd come face-to-face with Love. I just stared, gaping really, sincerely wondering at this peculiar and precious person. She knew something about the mercy of God that I certainly didn't.

She lowered her voice and spoke with deliberate peace. "God has forgiven me of so much, and I know He forgives you, too."

She refreshed her smile and my soul with her words of grace. From the weathered deck of my driven ship, I could see in her face the safe, warm glow of the lights of home.

"I asked God to forgive me," I confided. "I hope that He will—"

"No, He has!" Wendy interrupted with assurance. "If you've asked Him, He did what He said He would do. He doesn't lie."

"Okay." I tried to believe it. "No more drugs. No more drinking. No more lying," I promised from my heart.

"I do love God, you know. And I love you."

God had treated me with such kindness and grace. I couldn't believe it, nor could I ignore it. Wendy was right. He had done just what He said He would do.

Like the father of the prodigal, when his selfish and broken son returned home. When I made one step toward God, He ran passionately toward me and surrounded me with favor. His heart full of love, He had been waiting and watching for me to appear on the horizon of His hope.

When I cried out to Him, He was there. He answered with amazing grace and great power!

As you will see.

And to all the pirates who have targeted my ship, threatened my life, my purpose, and my destiny, I want to say clearly and boldly to your face: I'm alive. In Jesus Christ, I'm alive, forgiven, delivered, restored, empowered, and reconciled to my Father and His abiding unconquerable presence.

And to all my fellow travelers, I want to clearly and boldly say to you: If God has done this for me, He will do it for anyone.

THE BANNER OF THE KING

*Pirates strangled the life from their victims through oppressive control
and unimaginable violence distilled to its essence: torture,
both physical and mental. They could easily overpower their prey
with their sheer numbers of thugs alone. But their unified,
ever-intensifying devilry fostered an insatiable bloodlust.*

*Stunned sailors—captains and deckhands alike—were defenseless
against the man-o'-war ships the marauders had refitted specifically for
pirating. Dozens of cannons, flintlock pistols, whirling Knipple shot,
and a sword or dagger in the hands of hundreds of bandits
smothering the target all at once.
In a word, pirates thrived in an atmosphere of war.*

Watch out!" I screamed, one hand death-gripping the dashboard and the
other throttling the door handle.

Cracked and crackled, our soot-smeared windshield couldn't shield
my view of the oncoming massive grill of the eighteen-wheeler hurling
by, an inch or two from the front of our 1989 Skoda.

Ka-thunk! At the exact instant, when the mammoth truck was just
about on top of us, we plummeted into a rattle-your-teeth pothole,
lurching us even closer to the semi. I don't know how it missed us. With
my heart in my mouth and a noticeable ache in my neck, I flashed a
quick and questioning glance at my Romanian driver.

*Either he really knows what he's doing, or he's gone manic and is
going to get us killed!*

"Sorry," he said casually, one of the few English words he'd learned
while transporting tourists and missionaries. Unyielding, he sneered,

wagged his head, and sped up, only to continue swerving in and out of trucks and vans that were, *a incetini* (too slow).

"Is it always like this?" I asked, searching desperately for any semblance of a yellow line, white dashes, reflectors, *anything* to give me hope that I would make it to my hotel in one piece.

After driving around the towns of this oppressed formerly Communist country for a few days, I was convinced there were no specific laws governing their roads. Gradually, I became more comfortable with the chaos, but some of the heart-juddering close calls have stayed with me all these years.

Similarly, it felt as though much of the culture had been shaped by lawlessness, by the whims and moods of the dictators who, for the last century, had held sway over the helm of this sovereign state.

In 1999, when I visited my friends in Bucharest, Romania was still reeling from the tyrannical and destructive rule of a communist-governed coalition. It was primarily controlled by the Communist Party's general secretary, Nicolae Ceaușescu, from 1965 to 1989.

Prepping to visit the country for a two-week, multicity mission trip, I had read in an article that, through cruel and oppressive measures, Ceaușescu, Romania's last communist leader, and his administration had sought to dominate the people.

Like the menacing clouds of ash and carbon festering from many towering piles of burning tires, plastics, and other debris, hanging low over the cityscape bedimming any sparkle of lights, the heavy-handed rule of the Securitate, known as the most ruthless police force in the Eastern bloc, overshadowed the entire region with fear and subjugation.

On Christmas Day 1989, during the Romanian Revolution, Nicolae and his wife, Elena, were executed by a firing squad, launching the time-and-power-worn country into the swiftly modernizing global community, for which it wasn't at all prepared.

At different places and times throughout my visit, adhering to the updated and unspoken rules of hospitality toward tourists, small bands of uniformed police would daily gather at a distance to observe our fellowship as though looking for some reason to prevent us.

"Ce faci aici?"— "What is it that you're doing here, in Bucharest?"—one of the concerned *polițist* hollered from the huddle. The small cluster of constabulary glared collectively through their heavy cigarette smoke, waiting for an explanation.

"These are my friends, visiting from America," our host responded amiably, in perfect Romanian.

The group chuckled spuriously, looking around their circle and nodding at each other.

"Doar o vizit?!" "Only a visit!" The one who had questioned our presence jutted his jaw and tossed his head high as he gently patted his billy club. After a long and genuinely terrifying glare, they went back to their own conversations but never let us out of their view.

I'm sure it wasn't the case, but it seemed like everyone in Bucharest was a chain smoker. So, even though it was wet and cold, most afternoons we sat outside to drink our coffee. Inside the cafes, the tiniest, airless, windowless sitting rooms stuffed with artificial heat and lung poison were entirely suffocating.

During my entire sixteen-day trip to Eastern Europe, I didn't see a sliver of blue overhead; all seemed, at best, sepia. Once referred to as the Paris of the East, Bucharest was rigid and vapid. Except for a few small signs suggesting the businesses operating inside, every building in sight, dozens of them, were blanched a musty gray at the top and, as if being sucked down to a grave, blackened at the bottom with dirt and soot.

One afternoon, over the brim of my mug of *filtru*, topped heavily with *kaymak*, I watched a pack of dogs with wonder and concern. My ash-blurred eyes focused in on a good-size pack of emaciated feral dogs who were obviously hungry, haunched, and sizing us up.

"There're thousands and thousands of 'em," my host whispered his explanation. "Lots of them are insane because of hunger and disease, from drinking dirty water."

"Where'd they come from? Why are there so many?"

"When Ceaușescu leveled different parts of our city, thousands of families were driven from their homes. When they were displaced, so were their animals. The dogs, they're everywhere."

As I reached into my pocket to take out my *leu* to pay for our coffee and *kifla*, I recalled his earlier instructions.

"You should spread your cash out into different pockets. That way you can pull out only a bit at a time." He glanced to the left and to the right and offered, "People watch Americans because they always have too much money."

Mildly insulted, I scrunched my lips and nodded with intrigue and compliance.

"As well," he casually continued, "be sure your wallet is always at the bottom of your front pocket. Oh, and never wear your watch. Put it in your front pocket, too."

Everything was fragile, panicky, combustible, not only in a physical sense but spiritually and emotionally. I had stepped into a culture that had endured dominance, instability, suppression, and scarcity at the hands of iron-fisted tyrants for decades, which was clawing its way to freedom.

Other than law enforcement, most walked with their heads down as though they had a long way to go and a short time to get there. On a larger scale, the entire country, bordered by Ukraine and Moldova to the north, the Black Sea to the east, Serbia to the west, and Bulgaria to the south, was walking along the bladed edge of a steep social crevice, teetering with uncertainty; one misstep either way, and there was no telling where it would fall.

I learned so much while I was there and thoroughly enjoyed visiting with my friends. But on my last day there, with the last night that I would sleep in that cold and stony hotel on my horizon, I was ecstatic. I was beyond ready to go home. Spiritually, emotionally, physically, and socially, I felt as though I'd endured a different kind of keelhauling.

Early on the morning of my departure, as I was scooting along in a slow-moving line, pushing forward to board my US-bound airplane, the sullen and scowling faces of the PSP (public safety police) startled and would haunt me for some time.

You may have been admitted here, but you are not accepted here. You were not, and are not welcomed.

Shoulders hunched and head down, I pretended to be engrossed in my boarding pass. I did the best I could to avoid eye contact. Only slightly, I began to understand the downward cast of the population milling around me.

To say Communist-recovering Romania was dreary and dreadful is an understatement. I'm gladdened to know that over the last twenty years the quality of life for her citizens and the experience for their visitors has improved considerably. As much as my time there, and in other parts of Eastern Europe, impacted my life, it was during my trip home to America when I was most deeply impressed.

Welcome Home

Doesn't deboarding, especially after a fourteen-hour trip, feel like it takes nearly as long as the flight itself? I was at the back of the packed plane but so glad to be on the ground and thankful to hear the recorded announcements in my native language.

With my passport and all the necessary documents in hand, I winded my way through the endless and guarded hallways of Customs at JFK in New York. Even with dense gun-toting security, it affected me differently.

Can you remember, after you've been on a sugar bust for a couple of weeks, the moment you take your first bite of a fresh juicy orange? In the same sense, I was ultra-sensitive to all I was seeing and hearing. In a dreamlike way, I had been both transported and translated.

For sixteen days, at least emotionally if not literally, I'd been on lock-down in a colorless, broken, suffering world. No sunlight nor hint of ease or privilege.

Stay on your guard.
Don't look there.
Don't go there.
Don't touch that.
Don't laugh or talk too loud.

I realize America is far from perfect, but even our worst enemies acknowledge we are a blessed and favored people. As I walked into the US Customs Pavilion, everything seemed so spacious and gracious. The atmosphere was charged with promise, possibilities, and potential. I was overcome with an acute awareness of and appreciation for the blood-bought freedoms I had, for most of my life, taken for granted.

"Sir, you're next." The distinguished agent smiled and waved me through to the US Citizen's Entry. "Window number seven, please."

The attending CBP officer watched my exhausted approach to his desk at window number seven. His squinting gaze, at once firm and friendly, struck me and has stayed with me for all these years.

You are welcome here; you belong. Our protocol is for your protection and honor. I'm here to ensure you have what you need and to take from you what may harm others.

After a searing study of my passport and a line of direct questions, this resolute representative of Homeland Security caught me by surprise.

I'll always remember the feeling I had as he handed me my documents and included a business-card-size American flag and said, "Mr. Evans, the President of the United States and I welcome you home!"

All at once, I was humbled and proud, thankful, and inspired.

I wasn't exhausted anymore. I was invigorated.

I shifted my shoulders back and lifted my chest and chin high as I walked out of Customs and into the massive flow of humanity.

I hadn't reached my final destination, but I was where I belonged.

I was in my own country.

I was welcomed and wanted.

I was under the protection and favor of my country's covenant, the Constitution.

I was safe.

I was home.

It certainly seems illogical, but it was when I was surrounded by chaos and lawlessness that I felt the most confined and limited. The moment I stepped into order and structure, I walked into the gracious freedom all humans are created to expect and experience. This is what happens the moment you ask Jesus Christ to be your Savior and Deliverer.

He steps on board and immediately dethrones and deposes the pirate from your ship. As the Captain of your Salvation, He rips down Satan's prevailing death-doomed pennon and in its place raises His blood-bought, blood-stained banner of Life, Love, and Liberty. He restores your manifest and all that was lost under the pirate's tyrannical rule. When you invite the Son of God to take the helm of your life, He realigns your destination toward the warm lights of your eternal home, the shores of the city whose architect and builder is God.

"Arthur," I can hear Jesus saying, "the Father, His Holy Spirit, all of heaven, and I welcome you home!"

The Banner of the King

Raising the flag of the King of Glory over your ship changes everything! It is the most profound and pivotal expression of heart you'll ever make. In doing so, you're embracing and exalting Life Himself. In response to your trusting Him, God's Spirit makes a darkness-dispelling exchange: for your broken, depleted, and dominated heart, He gives you His rich, abundant, and liberating Life. Just as Jesus said, "The pirate comes only in order to steal and kill and destroy. I came that you may have and enjoy life, and have it in abundance (to the full, till it overflows)."

And there's more, much more, of great consequence. Please allow me to leave with you a few promises from God's Life-giving, life-transforming Word.

The Bible makes this bold and blessed declaration: "He who is joined to the Lord is one spirit with Him." As the Prince of Life takes His rightful place on your vessel, His Spirit and your spirit become one. In this miraculous union, all God is, and all God has is joined in your new heart.

"For in Him, the whole fullness of Deity (the Godhead) continues to dwell in bodily form [giving complete expression of the divine nature]. And you are in Him, made full and having come to the fullness of life [in Christ you too are filled with the Godhead—Father, Son, and Holy Spirit—and reach full spiritual stature]. And He is the Head of all rule and authority [of every angelic principality and power]." —Colossians 2:9-10 (AMPC)

By flying His colors, you're declaring to all other ships—private, public and pirate—who Jesus Christ is and all that He's done for you: (each bullet point is the Christian Flag)

149

- *This ship, this life, this destiny belongs to the Son of the Living God!*
- *I am redeemed by the Lord. God has taken my life out of the hand of the enemy!*
- *Jesus alone is the Hope of my life and heaven to come!*
- *I am forgiven of all my sins, and the power of iniquity is broken from my life.*
- *Every stain of shame and guilt is washed away.*
- *I'm a new creation in Christ! Old things have passed away, and all things have become new.*
- *I'm no longer my own but have been bought with the price of Jesus's own blood!*
- *As an heir of God and joint heir with Jesus, every promise and privilege is mine.*
- *My Savior, Redeemer, Healer, Provider, and Protector reigns in me.*
- *I'll never be alone again. I'm surrounded by heaven's hosts and the family of God.*
- *I am in Christ, and He is in me. In Him, I live, and move, and have my very being.*
- *I'm born of God, redeemed from darkness, and I'm heaven bound.*

The Spirit of Faith

Included in this sublime and miraculous union He makes between His Spirit and yours, God has proclaimed that everything He has belongs to you. As benevolent as this promise is, there's a higher gift yet: He has promised to give you Himself.

As one who is born of God, consider this: the Creator of everything, Who holds all wisdom, knowledge, and understanding; Whose insights and foresight are with perfect clarity; He Who is the Source of all strength and power, authority and might; He now lives in you, united with your heart! Indeed, the most victorious Warrior, the greatest resolute pirate punisher of all time and eternity has redeemed and joined Himself to your ship. He has generously included you in His triumph, His Kingdom, and world-loving cause.

All of this is possible because of God's unchanging love for you. I encourage you, into every area of your life and onto every deck of your ship, maximize this grace and generosity He has shown you. If you haven't already, take a moment and welcome Jesus, the Son of God and the Son of Man, to raise His flag over your precious life.

You need not yield a moment longer to the pirate, not to his presence, his plans, or his power. He's a vanquished foe. I like to visualize the Prince of Darkness this way: he's been dethroned, defeated, disarmed, and detoothed. The pirate has lost his bite, his power, and doesn't even have a leg to stand on.

Here's how the oracle Isaiah said it: "Oh Lord, You are our God. Other masters, besides You, have ruled and driven us, but now, we will acknowledge and mention Your great name only! They, the former tyrant masters, the pirates, are dead. They will not live nor reappear. They are the powerless ghost who will never rise nor come back; for You have made an end of them and their rule. You have caused every memory of them, every trace of their former supremacy to vanish. You are our Great Redeemer!" (Isaiah 26:13-14)

All the pirate can do now is, well, work like the devil to deceive, hoping you'll buy into his lies. You'll not be ensnared in his traps, though, because the Spirit of Truth lives in your heart, protecting and guiding you through both peaceful and troubled waters.

When you allow Him to raise His flag over your life, another gift His abiding Spirit imparts to your heart is what is called the Spirit of Faith. We might even call the spirit of faith the spirit of fight! When the robber tries to break in, or the deceiver advances to bargain with you, or the Tempter to entice, the Spirit of Might will rise up within you as a strong, fortified Defense!

He'll steadfastly remind you of your Father's promises and empower you to stand in your blood-bought victory and freedom.

"You are strong in the Lord and the power of His might," You'll hear Him declare. "You are Mine! And every child of Mine defeats this evil world as You trust and sail with Me through these chaotic and clamorous waters."

The shepherd boy, David, would be the first to tell you his triumph over the experienced, clothed-in-armor, fully armed giant Goliath was God's doing, not his. Yes, David slung the stone, but listen to what he had appropriately and accurately declared to his foul foe:

"You come to me with your sword and spear, but I come to you in the name of the Lord of Host, the God Who reigns in power on high; He, the One Whom you have defiled.

Today, the Lord will deliver you into my hand. I will pummel you and cut off your head. Then, I'm going to give yours, and the corpses of the army of Philistines, to the birds of the air and the wild beasts of the earth.

All the earth will know there is One God Who saves! The battle is the Lord's, and He'll give you into my hands." (1 Samuel 17:45-46)

Boethos!

If Jesus Christ had a ship, I'd like to think it would be called *Boethos.* This is the redemptive name the writer of Hebrews uses in referring to God as our Helper. Let these words of promise from our Champion, Who cannot lie, cannot fail, and will not deny your trust in Him, strengthen your heart:

> *For He [God] Himself has said, I will not in any way fail you nor give you up nor leave you without support. [I will] not, [I will] not, [I will] not in any degree leave you helpless nor forsake nor let [you] down [relax My hold on you]! Assuredly not!*
>
> *So we take comfort and are encouraged and confidently and boldly say, The Lord is my **Helper;** I will not be seized with alarm [I will not fear or dread or be terrified]. —Hebrews 13:5-6 (AMPC)*

Boethos: A ship laden with all supplies and artillery necessary to deliver, support, and protect.

The word picture the Bible gives us by assigning the title of *Boethos* to God is, He's like an anti-pirate naval warship: unstoppable, damage resilient, heavily armed, abundantly supplied, and authorized to strike.

Relentlessly scanning the horizon, Nissi (the Lord our Banner of Victory) is looking for anyone to whom He can show His strength, grace, and abilities.

Our Rescuer, Jesus Christ, is no fair-weather friend. He doesn't come and go as one whom you're never quite sure you can depend on. He's made a reputation for Himself throughout the ages as One Who stays closer than a brother and as a Helper Who can be counted on in times of trouble.

> *I will answer your cry for help every time you pray, and you will find and feel My presence even in your time of pressure and trouble. I will be your Glorious Hero and give you a feast. — Psalm 91:15 (TPT)[5]*

> *And therefore the Lord [earnestly] waits [expecting, looking, and longing] to be gracious to you; and therefore He lifts Himself up, that He may have mercy on you and show loving-kindness to you.*

> *For the Lord is a God of justice. Blessed [happy, fortunate, to be envied] are all those who [earnestly] wait for Him, who expect and look and long for Him [for His victory, His favor, His love, His peace, His joy, and His matchless, unbroken companionship]! —Isaiah 30:18 (AMPC)[6]*

It is essential for us to always remember, "We love God because He first loved us." He doesn't love us because we are loveable or good. He desires us because *He is good and He is Love*. His unrivaled, one-of-a-kind love, accepted into our hearts the moment we raise His flag over our lives, makes us loveable and capable of loving others. I believe real transformation is found in the fathomless depths of God's love.

I'm immensely grateful, even when I ignored Him and hardened my heart, He kept His gracious hand upon my life. I'm forever thankful He didn't leave me where He found me! And He didn't do this just for me.

What Jesus Christ has accomplished for one He has done for all. He's not a respecter of persons. He isn't partial to a particular position, personality, or pedigree. He isn't scanning the horizon looking for a specific type of community or religious group to help. He hasn't reserved or released His mercy toward people because of their skin color, age, or financial situation.

He's looking for any human who will acknowledge their need of Him and, by faith, cry out for His able, willing, and faithful help. To that person He has promised, *I'll be there!*

Personal Proclamation

Made in the image and likeness of your Creator, you have a God-given passion for life and freedom. This divine craving—this fire in your bones—can only be satisfied by grabbing hold of and experiencing the power, presence, and purpose of God found only in Jesus Christ!

No human has ever existed or ever will whom God intended to navigate this world apart from Him. Within Him alone are all the essential elements we need to defeat and dispel the pirates, thrive in this world, and one day arrive at the portals of heaven.

We need not muddle through this journey in fear, depression, regret, and exhaustion while leaving our eternal destination as little more than a wispy idea or the lucky roll of the dice.

As the captain of your ship, take decisive action over your life, your destiny. I encourage you to lift your heart and voice and boldly declare:

Jesus Christ, Prince of Life,
I ask You to raise Your Flag over my life. All that I am,
all that I have, and all I ever hope to become, I yield to Your Lordship.
I sail with You now, as the Captain of my Salvation.

Thank You for forgiving me of all my sins
and shattering the binding chains of iniquities.

Thank You for setting me free from every principality, pirate,
and stronghold, from all the powers of darkness.

Thank You for removing from my soul
every stain of shame, guilt, and condemnation.

Thank You for promising me that
You'll never leave me or forsake me but
You will always rise up to help me and cause me to overcome.

Thank You for restoring Your manifest for my life.
I'll hear Your voice and follow Your lead all the days of my life.
I trust You to guide me as we navigate the waters of this world.

Thank You for giving me Your Word, Your Name, Your Spirit, and all
the unstoppable spiritual weapons of warfare to defeat the
Prince of Pirates and all his regiments.

Thank You for writing my name in Your Lamb's Book of Life and for
Your promise that when I pass from this life, I'll immediately
and forever be in Your loving presence.

Thank You for setting into my heart the warm glow of Eternity that
graciously draws me to my final port of Heaven.

****

Now, to every pirate: In the name of Jesus Christ, I boldly proclaim,
your presence and power over my life, my family,
and my future are broken.

Your flags of death, darkness, doom, and despair—each and every one
of your tags—have been forever removed from my soul and
you'll never have me on the hook again.

I will not cower. I will not be silent. I will not fall prey.
I will give you no footholds; you will have no strongholds.

I will not spend the balance of my life running from the thief!
I will turn and confront every pirate that targets my ship.

Let them run from the Captain of my Salvation and from me!
Greater is the One Who sails with me than he who is against me!

For it is the blood-bought, blood-stained banner of
Jesus Christ under which I now sail.

So [as the result of the Messiah's intervention] they shall
[reverently] fear the name of the Lord from the west,
and His glory from the rising of the sun.
When the enemy shall come in like a flood,
the Spirit of the Lord will lift up a standard [flag] against him
and put him to flight [for He will come like a rushing stream
which the breath of the Lord drives].
Isaiah 59:19 (AMPC)

It is the blood-bought, salvation-securing, Life-giving, pirate-routing,
heaven-backing, Kingdom-representing, God-glorifying flag of
Jesus Christ flying over my life!

This flag does not come down!

ENDNOTES

1 "Blackbeard." *Encyclopedia of World Biography.* Encyclopedia.com: http://www.encyclopedia.com.

2 Crime Museum, LLC, All Rights Reserved, 2017.

3 Spence, L. (1993). *An Encyclopedia of Occultism.* Carol Publishing, New York.

4 William Cosmo Monkhouse, Poemhunter.com

5 The Passion Translation (TPT) Copyright © 2017 by BroadStreet Publishing® Group, LLC. Used by permission. All rights reserved. thePassionTranslation.com.

6 Amplified Bible, Classic Edition (AMPC) Copyright © 1954, 1958, 1962, 1964, 1965, 1987 by The Lockman Foundation.

Made in the USA
Las Vegas, NV
25 March 2021